THE
NORTHERN GULF ISLANDS
EXPLORER

THE•OUTDOOR•GUIDE

THE
NORTHERN GULF ISLANDS

EXPLORER

THE • OUTDOOR • GUIDE

Elaine Jones

WHITECAP BOOKS

Vancouver/Toronto

Edited by Bruce Obee

Cover photographs by Bob Herger
Photographs on pages 9, 24, 54, 56, 59 by Bruce Obee
Photographs on pages 113, 143 by Nick Lawlor
All other photographs by Elaine Jones

Maps by Jay Page

Cover design by Carolyn Deby

Typography by CompuType, Vancouver, B.C.
Printed and bound in Canada by Friesen Printers, Altona, Manitoba

Canadian Cataloguing in Publication Data

Jones, Elaine
    The northern Gulf Islands explorer

    Includes index.
    ISBN 1-895099-41-2

    1. Gulf Islands (B.C.) — Description and travel — Guide-books.
    I. Title.
FC3845.G8J65 1991   917.11'28044   C91-091067-7
F1089.G8J65 1991

Published by
Whitecap Books
1086 West 3rd Street
North Vancouver, B.C.
V7P 3J6

Cover: *Sandstone sculptures on Hornby Island.*

To David, Linnea and Jed

C O N T E N T S

Chapter Three:
Newcastle Island —
A Varied Past 51

Chapter Four:
Lasqueti Island —
A Rhythm of its Own 62

Chapter Five:
Denman Island —
An Easy Pace 77

A C K N O W L E D G E M E N T S

Thanks to the following people who helped in many ways ... Nancy Duggan for hiking and paddling Hornby with me; Mike Richmond of Abyssal Diving; Jason Puddifoot, and especially Jack Van Hove, for scuba diving background; Peter Mustard for providing information on rocks; Bill Grutzmacher of Fletcher Challenge for help with Quadra trails; Annemarie Koch; Jay Page; Rob and Bev Knight; Jim Emerson; Bob Herger; Dorothy Parkin; and Robert Fox; Whitecap publisher Colleen MacMillan for her encouragement; Bruce Obee for generously sharing his knowledge of the coast and for setting high standards; my family for memorable camping trips and their forebearance and support during the writing of this book; and David Parkin for being a patient, supportive and entertaining companion, on the road and at home.

PREFACE

I first came to this coast in the mid-1960s, after spending my early years on the Canadian prairies and a few years "back east." As soon as I reached the shores of British Columbia, I knew I had come home.

The wet, rich environment of the coast, the flux of the tides and the abundance and variety of life at the edge of the sea were endlessly fascinating. Like a five-year-old, I wanted to turn over rocks at the beach, collect sticks, bones, stones and shells, jump waves, dive at night to watch the play of phosphorescence in the water.

Over the years, much of my spare time has been spent exploring the coastal areas, for some years with three children in tow and a large canvas tent that we obstinately packed in to walk-in campsites. Lately I've streamlined my approach — no children and a dome tent that is miraculously easy and light to pack up. In all the years, the fascination has not waned one bit. I still catch my breath with the beauty of a sunset over water, marvel at the seasonal movements of wildlife and waterfowl, breathe deeply of the bouquet at low tide, and remain thankful that I fetched up on these shores.

The information in this book is the result of my experience exploring the islands, talking to residents and travellers, and collecting and reading what has already been written. The result is a mixture of fact and opinion that I hope you will use as a basis for your own explorations and discoveries on these beautiful islands.

The Northern Gulf Islands

Out of the Mainstream

 If a whiff of sun-warmed creosote gives you a thrill of pleasurable expectation, then you, too, are an islands traveller. The ritual of the passage — the ferry chugging into the dock and disgorging its passengers, the jockeying of vehicles to utilize every inch of space, the wheeling and crying of gulls, and the fresh salt air of the channel crossings — gives an added cachet to the sense of promise all travellers experience as they set out on a journey.

Perhaps part of the attraction of islands is the pace of life. Buffered by that saltwater crossing from the hurried tempo that elsewhere governs human activity, many islands operate on "island time." This can be

QUEEN CHARLOTTE STRAIT

MALCOLM ISLAND

CORMORANT ISLAND

Port McNeill

190 km

VANCOUV

PACIFIC OCEAN

Legend

▼ Ferry Terminal

Scale:

0 km   20 km   40 km   60 km   80 km

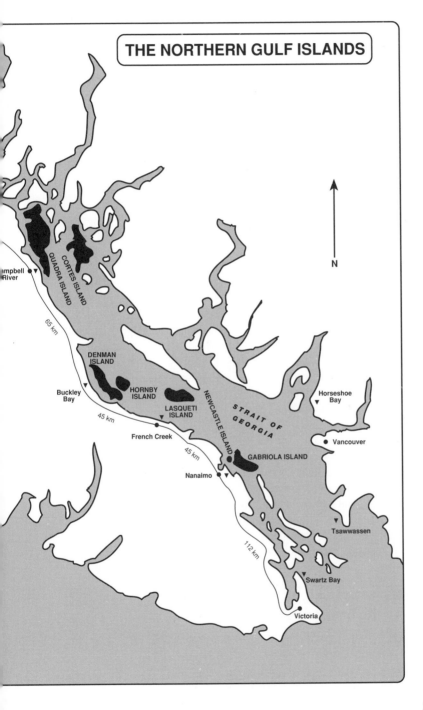

THE NORTHERN GULF ISLANDS

N

ampbell
River

QUADRA ISLAND

CORTES ISLAND

65 km

DENMAN
ISLAND

Buckley
Bay

HORNBY
ISLAND

LASQUETI
ISLAND

NEWCASTLE ISLAND

STRAIT OF
GEORGIA

Horseshoe
Bay

45 km

French Creek

45 km

Vancouver

Nanaimo

GABRIOLA ISLAND

Tsawwassen

112 km

Swartz Bay

Victoria

variously charming or highly aggravating; travellers are well advised to relax and find it charming.

Why these northern islands? First, they are all reached by ferry from Vancouver Island. That makes them accessible to hikers, cyclists and car travellers — Newcastle and Lasqueti are the exceptions, as they have only foot-passenger ferries.

Second, these islands are not, for the most part, as well known as the southern Gulf Islands. Even those that have considerable tourism in the summer do not usually have the same problems with ferry lineups and overcrowding as better-known tourist destinations. In exchange for the pleasure of driving onto the ferry without a tremendous wait, visitors can often expect fewer services.

Travelling northward, there is an ever-increasing sense of nature's power. Even though clear-cuts and other signs of logging are seen everywhere on the coast, elsewhere human interference diminishes as you head north. There is a certain rawness to the land: wilderness areas increase in proportion to settled lands; pastoral farmlands disappear in favour of dense, second-growth forest and uninhabited shores; rough gravel roads outnumber the paved ones.

The islands in this book lie in the straits between Vancouver Island and the mainland, stretching from Nanaimo almost to the northern tip of the island. Strictly speaking, they are not all Gulf Islands: technically the Gulf Islands lie in the Strait of Georgia, off southeast Vancouver Island. (Thought by early explorers to be a gulf rather than a passage, the names Gulf of Georgia and Gulf Islands have stuck with the general populace.) Gabriola, Newcastle, Denman and Hornby lie in the Strait of Georgia. Quadra and Cortes lie between the Strait of Georgia and Johnstone Strait; and Malcolm and Cormorant are in Queen Charlotte Strait. B.C. Ferries designates all those islands in the northern strait and the passage to the tip of Vancouver Island as northern gulf islands, and for the sake of convenience, they are so designated in this book.

Ferry terminals to the islands from Vancouver Island are located at Nanaimo, French Creek (just north of Parksville), Buckley Bay, Campbell River and Port McNeill. Travelling between the islands can be accomplished in small hops going up-island. In spite of fairly wide cultural and physical differences, the distances between the islands are not overwhelming — a total of 350 kilometres between the most southerly terminal at Nanaimo and the most northerly at Port McNeill. Of course, the Vancouver Island portion of these travels is interesting in itself .... but that is another book.

The Land — Rain Forests, Grasslands and Wildflowers

You may have a number of reasons for travelling on the islands, but one of them is certain to be an appreciation of their natural beauty.

Influenced by latitude and proximity to mountain ranges on Vancouver Island and the mainland, the islands vary somewhat in flora and fauna, topography, climate and even water temperature. They are generally low-lying, with isolated peaks not exceeding 340 metres. In the north, they are lower, flatter and more heavily wooded right down to the shore, with few large rocky outcroppings. Fresh water is at a premium in the southernmost islands, but Denman and Cortes have a number of lakes, and Quadra boasts the largest body of fresh water of any of the Gulf or Discovery islands.

Gabriola, Newcastle, Denman and Hornby are notable for their shoreline sandstone formations. They are often sculpted by wind and waves into smooth, rounded shapes that invite touching, flat slabs with perfect round holes, or lacy creations that look like frozen waves. These islands are part of the Georgia Basin, which includes the sedimentary rocks of the Greater Vancouver area, the southeast coast of Vancouver Island up to Courtenay, and the islands lying off this coast.

The rocks that form the islands discussed in this book are between 90 and 50 million years old. Erosion caused by geological forces over millions of years has produced sand, gravel and mud, which harden to become the sandstone, conglomerate and shale (also called mudstone) typical of the Gulf Islands.

Quadra and Cortes islands, to the north, mark the beginning of a

Sandstone formations at Tribune Bay, Hornby Island.

convoluted maze of islands and passages between Vancouver Island and the mainland. The inlets and narrows were once weaknesses in the rock, such as old faults and fractures, scoured out by ice during several glaciations in the last 200,000 years, drowned by rising seas after the last major ice sheets melted about 10,000 years ago, and eroded by waves and tides to become the waterways we know today.

Quadra Island is especially interesting to geologists because the island contains a major fault — a break in the underlying rock — which neatly divides the island into two vastly differing types of rock. If you drew a northeast-southwest line between Open Bay and Granite Bay, it would mark the fault, which separates the bedrock of Vancouver Island — mainly more than 200 million years old — from the rock of the mainland coast — mainly granites only 155 to 100 million years old.

The contact can be seen along the Open Bay shoreline, where the differing types of rock are visible; to the west are basaltic volcanic rocks, including pillow lavas; to the east are highly deformed shales and limestones intruded by granitic rocks. These mark the westernmost limit of the rocks common in the Coast Mountains.

The ecology of the islands varies from the rain forest typical of the entire B.C. coast to unique, dry, almost desertlike ecosystems found in isolated areas on Hornby and Lasqueti islands. An ecological reserve has been established on Lasqueti to protect the cactus and Rocky Mountain juniper that grow here in this dry zone.

Coastal travellers are often intrigued by the sensual, smooth limbs of the arbutus, which flourishes on Gabriola, Newcastle, Lasqueti, Denman and Hornby. Arbutus are said to grow "only within the smell of the ocean," and it is true that they grow close to the shore. Each spring, the deep red bark peels off in thin strips and new green bark is revealed, which turns red as summer progresses. The masses of white flowers produced in the spring become red berry clusters by fall. Arbutus grow best on dry, well-drained terrain, as do Garry oak, which are often found in the same location. Garry oak are distinguished by their deeply etched gray bark and twisted limbs. They are abundant on Newcastle and Gabriola, common on Hornby, Denman and Lasqueti, and unusual or nonexistent on the islands north of there.

The dominant tree species in the Georgia Strait region, Douglas fir is found on all the islands. Most of these trees are second growth, but many have attained considerable stature. A few monster firs can be seen at Helliwell Park on Hornby. Douglas firs thrive in dryer, warmer climates and are often found with arbutus and Garry oaks, and with an understory of salal, Oregon grape, huckleberry and sword fern in moist areas.

Farther north, western hemlock and red cedar dominate the forests. The tall cedars of Malcolm and Cormorant islands were sought for their straight true grain by the Kwakiutl, who used them for totem poles, ocean-going dugout canoes and other items. In fact, early coastal people relied on the cedar tree for almost every object in their everyday lives — from clothing, cooking utensils, storage boxes and baskets, to houses, mortuary poles, burial boxes and transportation. Today, cedar plays a significant role in the logging industry in the province, accounting for about 10 percent of the total annual cut for the province, and 25 percent of the coastal harvest.

Spring wildflowers — buttercups, monkeyflowers, larkspurs and sea blush — grow in profusion on dry bluffs and meadows, such as the cliffs at Helliwell Provincial Park on Hornby, the south end of Lasqueti Island and the islets surrounding it. Woodland flowers are more retiring. Pink fawn lily, Solomon's seal, fairy slipper, vetch and wood violet can be found hidden along forested trails. By the seashore there are glasswort, yellow sand verbena, sandwort, sea rocket and beach pea.

Wildlife — From Wild Sheep to Killer Whales

Land Mammals

The variety of habitats on the northern Gulf Islands allows a wide array of wildlife to flourish. Probably the most commonly sighted of the land mammals is the blacktail deer, which browses contentedly with domestic stock and is the bane of many island gardeners. Lasqueti Island also has a substantial population of feral sheep and goats, which behave in much the same way as the domestic varieties. Grazing side by side with tame sheep, they are distinguishable only by their long tails.

To the north, cougars and wolves inhabit the large unpopulated tracts

Deer and cattle on Cortes Island.

7

of land, but the large carnivores are seldom seen on islands south of Quadra and Cortes. Bears are a rare event, even in the north. Mink and river otters populate all the islands, and beavers have been reported on Newcastle and Denman.

Killer Whales

There are few sights more thrilling than a killer whale in the wild breaking the surface of the water. Many who frequent the coast have seen these large marine mammals — sometimes in an unexpected place, such as Vancouver's harbour, or off the bow of a ferry. Although they are sighted fairly frequently in Georgia Strait, they are most often seen in northern waters, particularly in the inlets and passages around Johnstone Strait.

The killer whale, also called orca, or blackfish in some coastal areas, is easily identified by its dramatic black and white colouring and large size. The male can be up to 10 metres in length; females generally grow to about 8 or more metres. Unlike many other large whales, the killer whale has not been a common target for whaling and the population has remained stable.

Scientists on the Pacific coast have been studying killer whales for over fifteen years. Using natural irregularities in dorsal fins and the area of white pigmentation behind the fin, they have identified all the whales that live in this area — some 330.

The whales fall into two groups: residents and transients. The residents live in large pods of five to fifty individuals. Primarily fish-eaters, they spend summer and fall in specific areas along the coast. The transients form smaller groups of one to five. They feed on marine mammals, such as seals, sea lions, porpoises and even larger whales, and are probably responsible for the killer whale's reputation for fierceness. The transients do not have a defined home area, but travel up and down the coast. Observations suggest that they avoid contact with resident whales.

Killer whales are highly social animals that appear to be playful in the water. Breaching, spy-hopping and tail-slapping may be part of this play, or they may have other purposes. Every year, killer whales come to their traditional rubbing beaches at Robson Bight in Johnstone Strait. The area has been designated an ecological reserve, and researchers follow the whales, taking advantage of the opportunity to study these intriguing mammals in the wild. Researchers are required to have a permit to study whales at the reserve.

Despite their name, killer whales are not known to be dangerous to humans. However, most people exercise good sense when in the water with a 6-tonne animal, and remain at a distance. The Canadian government has informal guidelines that suggest aircraft stay 450 metres above the water and that boats keep a distance of at least 100 metres from whales. Whale-watching tours have become popular in areas such as Johnstone Strait, and Fisheries and Oceans officials have been working with tour operators on whale-watching protocol. This growing industry may eventually be regulated through legislation.

Harbour Seals and Sea Lions

Paddlers on the coast often find they have a silent companion or two — harbour seals that parallel the boat, their sleek heads turning to observe your progress. They may disappear, only to bob up several minutes later, often at exactly the same distance from the boat. (Seals can remain submerged for almost half an hour.) Harbour seals are curious creatures, but they maintain their distance. Some seals become semitame when fed by boaters or divers, but most are extremely cautious; if you try to paddle closer to them, they will usually disappear.

Seals form family groupings and inhabit particular territories. In B.C. they can be seen year-round, particularly near rocky islands and islets, where they haul out and bask in the sun at low tide, the rising tide nudging them off their rocks to feed. Graceful and powerful in the water, they look somewhat ludicrous as they hump along on land.

Formerly hunted for bounty, seals became protected by law in 1970. Since then their numbers in B.C. have grown from 10,000 to more than 85,000 and are continuing to grow by over 10 percent a year. Recreational

Sea lions at a haulout.

9

boaters may enjoy the sight of these marine mammals, but commercial fishermen and fish farm operators are less enthusiastic. They believe that seals eat significant amounts of salmon and herring and destroy the nets of commercial fishing vessels and the sea pens at fish farms. A 1990 study of eating habits of harbour seals in the Strait of Georgia showed that herring comprises about 32 percent of a seal's diet — about one-quarter the amount of herring commercially caught each year. Salmon comprised only about 4 percent of the seal's diet. It's unlikely, however, that seals will lose their fascination for most people, who perhaps see human characteristics in the large limpid eyes and playful curiosity.

Sea lions are a larger relation of seals. The two species found in B.C. coastal waters are the California and the Steller's, or northern, sea lion. The Steller's sea lion is the largest of all: the biggest bulls can measure up to 4 metres in length and weigh a tonne. The females are much smaller, generally less than half the weight of the male. The Steller's sea lion was named *Leo marinus* — lion of the sea — by the German natural scientist, Georg Steller, who saw a resemblance to the lion in the powerful massive neck, slender hindquarters and golden-coloured eyes.

The Steller's sea lion breeds in rookeries in the north, where about 1,200 pups are whelped each year. This is just enough to keep the population at a stable 6,000 individuals. The females remain near the breeding grounds with the year's new brood. Only the males are seen in southern coastal waters, where they winter along the B.C. coast from September to April or May.

California sea lions winter in B.C. waters. They are darker in colour, a chocolate brown rather than the golden or auburn haired Steller's sea lion, and smaller. These sea lions are playful in the water, and can be seen tossing objects about much like the trained "seals" in circuses. The species is protected; in recent years California sea lions have been increasing in B.C. waters, causing some concern among other users of the waters.

For the Birds

When the surf scoters, buffleheads and horned grebes return to southern B.C. waters, it's a sure sign that summer is over. The annual migrations of birds that return from their northern nesting grounds to winter in coastal waters is one of the seasonal markers for coastal dwellers.

Trumpeter swans wintering on the B.C. coast concentrate in the Courtenay/Comox estuary area, but can be seen all along the coast. Some 3,000 are estimated to winter on the shores of Vancouver Island — 33 percent of the North American total, which is 90 percent of the world's population.

About 14 kinds of gulls are found in B.C. coastal waters, but the glaucous-winged gull is the most familiar of these, and the only species that breeds here. They are frequently seen on rocky islets with cormorants, which, along with pigeon guillemots, breed on the coast in the thousands.

The huge wing spread and gleaming head and tail of the bald eagle is a common sight all along the coast, but certain areas — where herring mill about in turbulent water, for instance — attract eagles in the dozens. Dodd Narrows and False Narrows near Gabriola Island, and the tidal channels around Quadra Island are two places where you can see huge concentrations of eagles. Other raptors include several species of hawk, which can be seen gliding over open meadow areas in search of mice and voles. Travellers are often surprised to see turkey vultures on the coast, yet the southern coast is one of two breeding areas in the province. They are commonly sighted in cliff areas, where they soar on the updrafts.

The great blue heron is always a fascinating sight. Herons frequent tidal lagoons, estuaries, marshes and docks, but they can be seen anywhere on inner coastal waters. The heron is patient, always moving in slow motion, almost immobile until it strikes like a snake. The epitome of elegance and grace as it stalks its prey by the water's edge, the heron's gawky, almost prehistoric appearance in flight and its indignant, croaking cry can be startling, particularly if you're quietly paddling along and unknowingly roust it. There are heron nesting sites on Gabriola and Hornby, but these sites do occasionally change.

Islands Weather — Be Prepared

Although the climate of these islands is moderated by the ocean currents, and they all lie in the rain shadow of the Vancouver Island ranges, rainfall and hours of sunshine are also determined by other factors, such as how far they lie from the mountains, prevailing wind systems, and latitude.

Visitors to the islands can usually expect a good share of sunshine in the summer, plenty of rain in the winter, and summer fog on Malcolm and Cormorant islands. Lasqueti has the driest conditions and Malcolm and Cormorant the wettest. But the best response to the weather is to throw out any expectations and be prepared for anything, especially on the northernmost of these islands. Those who can accept and even enjoy the varying moods of nature will have the best time. Carry rain gear in all seasons, and bear in mind that travelling outside the peak summer months can be more enjoyable in some cases — if you are prepared for the weather.

The following charts, based on statistics compiled over several decades at weather stations operated by Environment Canada, illustrate the temperature and precipitation a traveller can expect in some of the northern Gulf Islands. There aren't weather stations on all the islands. Alert Bay

(Cormorant Island) and Cortes are detailed here; the Comox weather station is representative of nearby Denman and Hornby islands. Temperatures are in Celsius, precipitation in centimetres.

Alert Bay

Temperature

	Jan	Feb	Mar	Apr	May	Jun	Jul	Aug	Sep	Oct	Nov	Dec
Mean:	2.8	4.6	5.2	7.4	10.2	12.3	14.0	14.3	12.6	9.3	5.7	3.9
Max:	4.7	6.9	8.2	11.1	14.3	16.0	17.8	18.1	16.1	12.0	7.7	5.7
Min:	.9	2.2	2.1	3.8	6.0	8.5	10.2	10.5	9.0	6.5	3.5	2.0

Precipitation

Jan	Feb	Mar	Apr	May	Jun	Jul	Aug	Sep	Oct	Nov	Dec
19.5	13.5	12.3	8.3	6.0	6.6	5.2	6.7	11.9	20.9	21.2	23.4

Cortes Island

Temperature

	Jan	Feb	Mar	Apr	May	Jun	Jul	Aug	Sep	Oct	Nov	Dec
Mean:	2.4	4.3	5.6	8.4	12.1	15.4	17.8	17.5	14.4	9.9	5.7	3.9
Max:	4.5	6.8	8.7	11.8	16.1	19.5	22.3	21.5	17.8	12.6	8.0	5.9
Min:	.2	1.7	2.4	4.9	8.1	11.3	13.3	13.5	10.9	7.2	3.4	1.8

Precipitation

Jan	Feb	Mar	Apr	May	Jun	Jul	Aug	Sep	Oct	Nov	Dec
16.8	12.8	11.7	7.3	6.3	5.6	4.5	6.1	8.4	15.9	18.8	20.8

Comox

Temperature

	Jan	Feb	Mar	Apr	May	Jun	Jul	Aug	Sep	Oct	Nov	Dec
Mean:	2.2	4.0	5.0	8.0	11.8	15.0	17.4	17.0	13.7	9.2	5.3	3.7
Max:	4.9	7.2	8.8	12.4	16.8	19.7	22.7	22.0	18.4	12.9	8.4	6.3
Min:	−.6	.9	1.2	3.6	6.8	10.2	12.1	11.9	9.0	5.4	2.3	.9

Precipitation

Jan	Feb	Mar	Apr	May	Jun	Jul	Aug	Sep	Oct	Nov	Dec
19.3	12.5	11.2	5.7	3.7	3.5	2.8	4.4	5.2	12.8	19.2	21.3

Information

B.C. is divided into nine tourism regions, each with its own association, listed in the telephone directory under tourism. The islands in this book fall into the Vancouver Island tourism region. Many businesses on the islands belong to the association, and information is available from their offices.

Travel Infocentres located at conspicuous sites in many communities are another good source of information on all areas of B.C. They are operated by chambers of commerce and municipalities, and have variable hours and locations depending on the fluctuations of the local economy. Some are open year-round at regular hours; others are seasonal. Ask at local businesses for the location of Infocentres, or watch for signs.

For information on services not listed with either of these sources, try calling businesses in the local telephone directory. Most are happy to provide travellers with information on their area.

Camping and Accommodation

Accommodations — both camping and indoor — are often extremely limited in the northern Gulf Islands. Only five of the islands covered here — Newcastle, Denman, Quadra, Cortes and Malcolm — have provincial or regional parks with public camping. None of these campgrounds accepts reservations, and some are very small, making chances of getting a site even less likely. A fee is charged in provincial campgrounds.

In addition to government campsites, many of the islands have commercial campgrounds, and marinas, charter businesses and other recreational facilities often have campsites. Reservations are accepted at most of these outlets and are highly recommended, at least for the first night. Once you are sure of accommodation on the island, you can check out other facilities and perhaps relocate if another campground seems more desirable.

Hotels, motels, inns, lodges and bed and breakfast accommodations

Campground at Bere Point Regional Park, Malcolm Island.

are available on all the islands (except Newcastle, which is entirely reserved as provincial parkland). The number, type and level of luxury of these accommodations varies vastly, but it is safe to assume that reservations are always a good idea, particularly in July and August, and during holiday periods at other times of the year. If you're travelling outside peak tourist times, be sure to check that accommodations are open year-round.

Accommodations change from year to year, and are not specifically listed in this book. Probably the best single source for current information on accommodations is Tourism B.C.'s *Accommodations* booklet, which is updated annually and lists hotels, motels, inns, lodges, campgrounds and some bed and breakfast establishments by geographical area. The booklet is available free at Travel Infocentres, government agents' offices, travel agencies and from the Tourism B.C. office. Information in the booklet is provided by the individual businesses and checked by government inspectors to ensure that the information is accurate and that they meet a common standard of comfort, cleanliness and courtesy. Not all accommodations are listed in *Accommodations*; some are new, others have not submitted the forms in time, and others may not have been approved.'

Police and Medical Services

The RCMP is responsible for policing the islands. Some islands have permanent detachments, while others are policed from Vancouver Island or nearby islands.

Medical and hospital facilities also vary from island to island; Alert Bay on Cormorant Island has a hospital, many islands have medical clinics with full- or part-time medical staff, and some have no medical facilities. The B.C. Ambulance Service, operated by the provincial government, has been in operation since 1974 and is the largest geographic ambulance service in the world. Ambulance services in British Columbia are operated through this organization.

If you dial an emergency number, your call is automatically call-forwarded to headquarters in Victoria and help is dispatched from there. In remote regions, medical services may not be as quickly obtained as they are in major cities. Where there is a life-threatening emergency, a hovercraft or aircraft may be sent to the island; in other cases, the ambulance will travel by ferry. Telephone operators in Victoria are paramedics who maintain telephone communication and provide emergency instructions until help arrives. In some cases, such as when weather conditions prevent access to an island, this telephone communication can mean the difference between life and death.

Emergency numbers for police, ambulance and fire departments are located at the front of telephone directories. In some parts of B.C. you can simply dial 911 in an emergency. During the 1990s, the 911 system may be implemented on some of the islands in this book. In an emergency, telephone operators can often help.

Rights, Responsibilities and Common Sense

Public Areas and Private Property

As more travellers discover the northern Gulf Islands, increasing demands are placed on the provincial and regional parks systems to provide areas for the public to enjoy. Recent years have seen the establishment of several new parks, but this increase has not kept up to the demands.

Locals who have traditionally used logging roads and carved out trails on Crown land have opened up more areas for public use. Some are detailed in this book, and residents can give information about others. However, well-known trails that islanders have used for generations may not necessarily be Crown land or parkland, so if you use them, be aware that you could be trespassing if you do not have the owner's permission. The hiking trails in this book cover only those trails in public areas.

With a few exceptions, all foreshore is public property to the highest high tide line. Often, this is the best way — or even the only way — to enjoy an area. In the summer, it is often possible — and within the public right — to camp below the high tide line, although camping on public beaches is discouraged in some places. On many of the islands, residents have made a point of clearly marking public access to waterfront.

All Indian Reserves are private land and should be treated accordingly. Occasionally, property owners let people use private property if permission is requested and care is taken. Where that permission is not granted, stay off.

The rights of property owners must be strictly respected, but the traveller should also remember that most Crown lands, including foreshore to the high tide line, belong to the public.

Fire!

Newcomers to the islands might not appreciate at first how serious a threat fire can be, particularly in the southern, drier islands. Tinder-dry forests, difficult terrain, and lack of available water and equipment is a deadly combination. A thoughtless act — improper extinguishing of a campfire, or tossing a cigarette butt onto a forest path — can set the stage for disaster.

More than 53 percent of all fires in British Columbia are due to human causes — and that means they are preventable. A good proportion of those are due to careless smokers. If you want to smoke while you're on a hike, take a rest break; in a dry forest, even a spark knocked from a cigarette end can be dangerous. A better rule of thumb in high-risk areas is to wait until you are in a safer place.

Campfires are permitted on Crown land, such as beaches below the high tide line. Under B.C. Forest Service regulations, a campfire must not be within 3 metres of stumps, logs, overhanging trees or buildings, or within 15 metres of flammable debris such as slash or dry grass. A space of 1 metre around the fire must be cleared of debris such as moss, and grass. The fire must not be more than a metre wide and a metre high, and a shovel or pail of water must be kept nearby. The fire must be extinguished so that the coals are cool enough to pick up with your bare hand.

Some areas are permanently closed to fires and are usually signposted. All fires are banned or restricted to designated areas when the fire risk is high, usually all of August and sometimes longer. Fire closures are posted at ferry terminals and fire halls throughout the islands, and fire wardens, usually volunteer, help to get the information out.

Fifty-five percent of fire reporting in B.C. is done by the public, so your involvement is essential to control fires. If you suspect or spot a forest fire, call the operator and ask for Zenith-5555, a toll-free number throughout British Columbia.

Petroglyphs — Messages from the Past

One of B.C.'s cultural heritages is the petroglyphs and pictographs — rock carvings and paintings — made by those native people who inhabited this area for thousands of years before Europeans explored these shores.

Very little is known about the age of the petroglyphs, who carved them, or why. Scientists postulate that petroglyphs may have been created at ceremonial sites and could have had spiritual or religious significance. Others think they may have been messages, either to other people or to unseen spirits. Some even speculate that at least some of the glyphs were a means of passing time, like doodling.

Most of the carvings and pictographs of the B.C. coast are impossible to date, although some are known to have been carved as recently as the 19th century. Archaeologists, geologists and anthropologists work together to make educated guesses, using styles of art and other clues to indicate age. It is possible that some are as old as 10,000 years, when archaeologists have dated the first settlements on the coast.

These sites are powerful messages from the past, evidence of a human presence stretching back through the centuries. Unfortunately, many have been tampered with, and the erosive forces of wind and wave have acted on others until they are barely visible.

In order to protect them from natural erosion, some petroglyph boulders have been placed under cover, such as those in a park at the Cape Mudge Indian Village on Quadra Island. Others are on private property, which may protect them from defacement by the public.

All petroglyphs are protected by law. The Heritage Conservation Act, enacted in 1979, sets stiff fines, jail terms, or a combination of both for anyone who should "destroy, deface or alter an Indian painting or carving on rock."

Some destruction is wanton vandalism, but other damage comes from ignorance. Some people — who may well appreciate the artistic and cultural value of the petroglyphs — have used chalk or crayon to outline the lines of the carvings before taking photographs. As well as being temporarily disfiguring, it contributes to erosion and is prohibited by law.

Others may have unwittingly contributed to erosion by taking rubbings of petroglyphs. Rubbings are made using a technique of stretching cloth or paper over the carving and lightly rubbing its surface with a crayon. It is now illegal to take petroglyph rubbings without first acquiring a permit. Information on permits and the law governing archaeological and historic sites is available from the Archaeology Branch of the provincial government, or the Royal British Columbia Museum, in Victoria.

Tracing the lines of a petroglyph with your hand, thinking of the carver who might have stood in this very spot, wondering and speculating on his

Deeply incised petroglyph.

17

thoughts creates a rare bond with the past. While we don't yet understand what petroglyphs might have signified to their creators, they may contain a key for unlocking secrets at some future time. It is important to protect that legacy for the future.

Archaeological Sites — Signs of the First People

The coast is dotted with archaeological sites containing the remnants of cultures that thrived here over the past several thousands of years. Many of these sites are within our public parks, and while they are not marked, they are often visible as layers of shells interspersed with earth.

The people who once lived here collected shellfish, smoked fish, made tools of stone, bone and wood, created art, built homes, had families, and lived and died on the land where we walk today. This lifestyle was essentially undisturbed for thousands of years until the last two centuries. Archaeologists have determined some of these activities from artifacts found in sites up and down the coast, adding a valuable piece to the puzzle of human history.

Avoid the temptation to disturb shell heaps or other sites if you come across them. Anyone doing so is liable to severe penalties. Under the Heritage Conservation Act (the same Act governing petroglyphs and pictographs), it is forbidden to "destroy, deface, alter, excavate, or dig in an Indian kitchen-midden, shell-heap, house-pit, cave, or other habitation site, or a cairn, mound, fortification or other site or object." The law protects the cultural history of native inhabitants of the coast today and preserves the sites for future generations.

B.C. Aquaculture — Home-grown Seafood

Visitors to the northern Gulf Islands are certain to encounter the B.C. aquaculture industry in one form or another. The western shores of Denman Island are lined with oyster leases and the northern parts of Quadra and Cortes islands provide excellent conditions for another fast-growing industry, production of domestic salmon.

Oyster Leases

Those who are tempted to walk on the oyster beds at foreshore leases may be surprised to know that it takes at least three years to get a seed oyster from that beach and onto the half shell at their favourite oyster bar.

The culture of Pacific oysters is the oldest aquaculture industry in B.C., going back to the 1950s and even earlier. As early as 1912, shellfish were being imported from Japan for cultivation in B.C. The oyster most of us are familiar with is descended from that early stock, which propagated and populated the coast. Our native B.C. oyster is much smaller and takes longer to grow than the Japanese variety. Oysters are sold in a variety of sizes; the smallest take fifteen to eighteen months to grow and the largest upwards of five years. Farmers usually harvest oysters at about three years.

There are two types of lease: the beach, or bottom culture, lease, which is the oldest method, and the more recent longline — off-bottom or deepwater — lease. In bottom culture, small oysters or seed are spread along the beach in the mid to lower intertidal zone, where they grow for three to five years before harvest. Much of the productive shoreline is already under tenure, and as the demand for Pacific oysters increases, longline leases are becoming more common. Longlines are offshore lines that are supported by flotation, such as plastic floats or barrels. The lines are usually heavy synthetic rope, often hundred of metres long. From them are suspended oyster trays or strings — lighter rope that may be several metres long. At intervals of about 30 centimetres, pieces of seeded cultch (old shell) are inserted between the strands of the rope. (The cultch is seeded in tanks and removed to a nursery area until the seed oysters are about 3 centimetres in diameter before being tied on the lines.) By the time the strings are dragged up, anywhere from eighteen months to three years later, they weigh 25 kilograms or more.

There are hundreds of oyster farms on the coast, many on the east coast of Vancouver Island from Nanoose Bay to Courtenay and on the northern Gulf Islands to Desolation Sound. Oysters are quite fussy about where they like to grow. Denman is a good oyster-growing area: the water is of a fairly constant, relatively warm temperature; there is an ample food supply in spring and summer; and the channel is relatively calm and protected from heavy storms, which can damage the lines, smash the young oysters or toss them up on the beach above the high tide line.

It is illegal to pick oysters from an oyster lease, of course, but it's all right to use the beach. The oyster beds will be lower on the beach, so keep close to the high tide line when walking where there are oyster leases, as the tiny oysters are easily crushed.

Fish Farms

Fish farming is an increasingly important industry on the coast, with a concentration of sites in and around northern Georgia Strait and the Desolation Sound area.

Intensive salmon farming began here in the 1980s, when an increasing market for Pacific salmon gave a boost to the new industry. It originated in Norway around the late '70s, based on data gathered in part from scientific research conducted in Canada.

The best condition for raising salmon is cold, rapidly moving water that is constantly flushing: the waters around Quadra Island are ideal. So far, the industry has concentrated on chinook salmon, followed by Atlantic salmon and coho. Commercial culture of sockeye is also being tested on the coast.

The salmon are kept in large rectangular pens made of fine netting, which are attached to a series of docks. These cages must be impenetrable to predators, such as seals, otters, herons and other birds. It's not uncommon to see herons perched on the docks, apparently gazing longingly through the nets at their unattainable prey.

Some operations have their own hatchery to produce brood stock, as well as sea cages, and processing and marketing operations. Smaller farms are more likely to buy brood stock from a supplier. It takes eighteen months to two years to grow salmon to market size, and farms generally have two to three age groupings in different pens, in order to keep a constant market supply. Often the age groupings are separated by a distance of a quarter-kilometre or more, in order to minimize transmission of disease.

Many salmon farmers are eager to explain their operations and encourage visitors who respect what they are trying to do. Some farms are quite isolated, and the farmers enjoy the company.

Salmon Enhancement Programs

As little as a hundred years ago, the coastal waters teemed with wildlife. Huge humpback whales were seen in the inside waters. Herring were so thick in the channels that it was said you could scoop them out with your hands. Spears and fish weirs were all that was needed to catch salmon that choked the water during spawning runs.

Today all that has changed. While B.C. coastal waters are still considered some of the best in the world for sport and food fisheries, regular closures of coastal areas to fishing have become a way of life for both anglers and commercial fishboat operators.

Since the late 1970s a concerted effort has been made to develop a salmonid enhancement program, with the goal of returning salmon stocks to their pre-1900 levels. A joint responsibility of federal and provincial officials, enhancement programs affect not only the five species of salmon, but also sea-run trout such as steelhead and cutthroat.

The activities of the program vary from clearing debris from natural spawning streams and building fishways and artificial spawning channels, to building hatcheries. Many of the projects are operated on a local level, with supervision and input from government officials. Travellers on the coast will see the evidence of this work along streams, which may be signposted as salmon spawning streams that are part of the salmonid enhancement program, and in hatcheries and other facilities, such as the hatchery on Quadra, which may be open to the public.

Paddling and Small Boating — Sheltered Bays, Turbulent Channels

Canoes, kayaks, cartoppers and boat trailers towed behind motor homes: the number of small craft heading out to the northern Gulf Islands testifies to the attraction of these waters for paddlers and small boaters — and it is indeed a paradise. There are secluded coves, sandy beaches, fantastic rock formations, and wildlife that ranges from curious seals to magnificent killer whales. In the distance, vast ocean vistas open up, or islands and peaks recede in shades of indigo that finally merge with the sky. It is possible to find a deserted cove with no other trace of human life, or to enjoy the company of like-minded voyagers in small maritime communities.

One of the best ways to explore any island is by small boat. It is ideal for investigating all the nooks and crannies of a convoluted coastline, navigating shallow lagoons and creeks, and beaching your craft to explore for awhile on land.

Boaters should only venture out with proper hydrographic charts and tide and current tables, available from local marinas and sporting goods stores as well as some bookstores. Always carry fresh water and emergency rations (even for a day paddle), matches in a waterproof container, a

Maze of channels in the Finnerty Islands near Lasqueti.

flashlight, flares, a bailing container and, of course, adequate flotation devices for everyone on board. With a basic knowledge of winds, tides and water safety, and informed use of tide and current tables (current tables are most important when dealing with constricted tidal rapids), much of the coastline of the islands described here can be safely enjoyed — with limitations.

The narrows of Gabriola and Quadra should be avoided. The tidal streams in Discovery Passage around Quadra Island are among the fastest in the world, running at rates up to 16 knots. In the constricted passages of Seymour Narrows and Surge Narrows, west and east of Quadra, yawning whirlpools can open suddenly, and metre-high overfalls and powerful back eddies are common. Even at slack tide, a brief period that may last from fifteen minutes to half an hour, the water never stops moving. These waters have claimed many lives, and while they are not impossible to navigate, they are only for expert boaters with local knowledge.

Even a 2- to 3-knot current can create problems — or at least a lot of extra work — for human-powered craft, and the wise paddler will understand the currents and plot a course that will utilize them to advantage.

Small boat operators should keep a watchful eye on the wind and always know where they can run for cover should a squall rise quickly. The long open passages of Georgia Strait to the south of Lasqueti, Hornby, Quadra and Cortes are particularly subject to sudden winds. Small riffles on the surface are usually precursors to a rising wind; distant clouds moving rapidly toward your location are also an indicator. The wind should always be considered in conjunction with the tidal currents; even a slight wind can kick up a dangerous chop when opposed to a strong tidal stream.

In most of the northern Gulf Islands, summer winds are predominantly west or northwestlies; about 20 percent of summer winds will come from the south or southeast. Winter brings the reverse. These wind patterns are associated with high and low pressure areas. The prevailing winds are also affected by the daily cycles of land and sea breezes caused by unequal heating and cooling of land and air masses. Morning is usually the calmest time, with breezes rising in the afternoon and fading before sunset. The breeze will probably pick up again during the night and fade with the dawn.

Distances for the boating sections are in nautical miles (all other distances in this book are in metres and kilometres). One nautical mile is equal to 1.85 kilometres.

Hypothermia

Anyone using a small craft on the coast runs a danger of being accidentally dumped in the sea. But many people don't realize that even in the hottest summer, water temperatures in many areas of the B.C. coast never exceed 10⁰ — a temperature that can kill a person in as little as one hour.

Except in tropical waters, where temperatures achieve 20 to 25°C, prolonged water immersion quickly lowers the inner body temperature from the normal level of 37.6°C, causing slowing of the heartbeat, reduced metabolic rate and an increase in the amount of carbon dioxide in the blood. The first sign of hypothermia is mental confusion, the disorientation often contributing to the problem because the victim cannot take the measures necessary for survival. Within an hour, unconsciousness may occur, as the body temperature is lowered to about 32°C. When the internal body temperature drops below 30 to 26°C, death is almost certain to follow.

For the areas discussed in this book, only rarely, under protected conditions, does water attain temperatures of 20°C. In restricted tidal passages, where upwellings of colder deep water keep the surface cold, and in open areas, where frequent strong winds disrupt the warm surface layer of the water, mixing it with colder water, temperatures remain as cold as 10°C, even in midsummer.

An average person's life expectancy in water of 5 to 10°C is 1 to 3 hours; unconsciousness will occur after 30 to 60 minutes. At 10 to 15°C it is 1 to 6 hours, with unconsciousness occurring after 1 to 2 hours. An average person can survive for up to 40 hours in water temperatures of 20 to 25⁰. These figures are affected by variables such as body mass and body fat ratio and age. Those with more body fat are less susceptible to hypothermia; a very thin person would have a significantly lower expectation of survival than the average figures given above. A child is more at risk than an adult of comparable body fat to mass ratio.

Studies of cold water immersion have shown there are several other factors that affect chances of survival in the water. Proper clothing, including a life jacket or "floater coat," and a knowledge of protective measures that can be taken in the water can be crucial to survival — in some cases doubling survival time. Even a few minutes can make a difference, if it is the time needed for help to arrive.

Unless shore is only a short distance — and this is difficult to judge — a person should not attempt to swim. Unlike situations on land, where activity may help to prevent heat loss, cooling occurs 35 percent faster in the water when people move around. The activity increases circulation of blood to the arms, legs and skin, where it is cooled by contact with the water.

Protection of the critical heat loss areas — the head and neck, sides of the chest and groin — can vastly increase survival time. Researchers at the University of Victoria developed the "Heat Escape Lessening Posture" (HELP) to conserve body heat: the upper arms are held tight against the chest, the knees are pressed together and raised to the chest. Studies show that this posture, which only works if the person is wearing a personal flotation device, can almost double the length of survival time.

Those who are not wearing a life jacket should not lie back in the floating posture; dog paddling in the upright position, even though it cools the body through exercise, is preferable to immersion of the head, the most crucial heat-loss area of the body.

Boaters should be prepared with warm clothing, including a woollen hat. It's a good idea, especially when there are children along, to pack an extra sweatsuit in plastic bags or airtight buckets. Getting dumped is not the only danger to boaters: heavy rain or a soaking from rough seas can also cause hypothermia.

If a victim of hypothermia cannot get immediate medical treatment, the following measures should be taken. Remove all wet clothing and cover the victim with warm dry blankets or a sleeping bag. It does no good to wrap the victim in blankets unless there is an outside source of heat, so apply hot, wet towels, or one or two people should strip and lie next to the victim, sandwich-style. Warming the outside of the victim without warming the interior organs can actually be harmful, as it can put an added strain on the heart. If possible, direct hot steam beneath a hood over the victim's head, or simply breathe in the area of the mouth and nostrils. Warm, nonalcoholic drinks will also help.

A boating accident can happen to anyone, and certain factors are immutable. But those who have the proper equipment and who arm

Fishing in the northern Gulf Islands is some of the best on the coast.

themselves with knowledge of cold water survival tactics are providing themselves with the best possible odds of survival.

Fishing and Shellfish Harvesting — Something for Everyone

For many people the coast is synonymous with fishing. Each year, when the mature salmon return to their spawning grounds, anglers congregate in the hot spots to try for the huge tyees that will seal their reputation among their peers. Bottomfish such as lingcod, rockfish and greenling, as well as winter chinook and resident salmon provide good eating throughout the year.

Every angler should have a copy of the current *B.C. Tidal Waters Sport Fishing Guide*. This booklet, available at sporting goods stores, marinas and government outlets, has up-to-date information on licences, limits, restrictions and closures — essential information for the angler, who is legally obliged to be informed as to his or her rights and responsibilities. It also contains information on subjects related to the sports fishery, such as enhancement programs, tagged fish, research programs, and fishing and safety tips.

Licences are required for everyone catching fin fish — including spear-fishing children and scuba divers. Licences are available from sporting goods stores and government agents. Boat rentals and excellent guiding services are available from some islands and out of Campbell River, where the tackle shops are an angler's dream.

Some of the islands have good-sized lakes, and trout fishing is a popular pastime on Denman, Quadra and Cortes islands. Trout in these lakes can reach sizes of 40 centimetres. Licences are required and are available from sporting goods stores and government agents.

Salmon and Bottomfish

Salmon is without doubt the favourite of B.C. coastal sports anglers and gourmet cooks. B.C. waters are home to five species of salmon: chinook, coho, chum, pink and sockeye. Salmon are anadromous, that is, they spawn in fresh water, but spend most of their adult life — from two to five years — in salt water. They spawn only once, returning to the exact place of their birth, and dying immediately afterwards. From June to September fishing is hottest on the coast, as mature fish gather to make their final journeys upstream to their spawning grounds.

Exactly how salmon find their own birthplace is still a mystery to scientists, but anglers don't worry about that; they simply make their own annual treks to where the salmon gather in the summer months.

Although the biological cycles are not completely predictable, salmon generally follow certain patterns. Pink salmon run in two-year cycles — being more abundant in northern waters in even-numbered years and in southern waters in odd-numbered years — and are the smallest of the salmon, usually weighing just over 2 kilograms and rarely exceeding 4.5. Coho weigh between 1.5 and 14 kilograms and are called bluebacks when they are passing from the grilse stage to maturity. Sockeye weigh between 2.2 and 3 kilograms. Chum, or dog salmon, resemble sockeye but are larger, at 4.5 to 6.5 kilograms. Chinook are the coveted prize of anglers. They weigh in at from 1.5 to 30 kilograms. Also known as springs, they are tyee when they attain weights of 13.5 kilograms or more.

Salmon are not the only reason to fish these waters. Near the rocky ledges and dropoffs, white fish such as· rockfish, cod, red snapper and other bottomfish can also be caught.

There are several good books written for anglers who want to know about the hot spots on the coast; anglers can also make their own deductions based on a general knowledge of the habits of finfish, a close look at the configuration of the land with the use of marine charts, and local knowledge of the tides and currents. Wherever local boats are congregating, gulls are wheeling or herring jumping, there will probably be plenty of fish.

Shellfish

There is something particularly satisfying about collecting your dinner from the seashore, preparing a good fire on the beach as the sun sets and cooking and eating your catch as the light fades and the sky fills with stars. All you need is a shovel for digging clams or a knife for opening oysters, a large pot (or simply a grate), a little butter and lemon, and perhaps a clove of garlic and a loaf of crusty French bread. You don't even need to have a boat in order to collect the basis for this gourmet meal.

Edible shellfish include clams, oysters, mussels, abalone, crabs and sea urchins — all of which can provide a hearty meal. Clams and oysters, abundant on the coast and easy to collect and prepare, are the choice of many campers. Before harvesting shellfish, check Fisheries regulations regarding size and catch limits.

Many years ago, you could have prepared your meal at practically any good shellfish location up and down the coast. Today many areas are occupied by oyster leases, which are off-limits to public picking. (However, a number of other areas have been set aside as public shellfish reserves, where there is no commercial picking.)

A more serious obstacle to random picking of shellfish is sewage and chemical contamination. This is most likely to occur in areas of high residential concentration or where industrial wastes are released into the water, such as around pulp mills. Programs to monitor contamination of shellfish have been established by the federal government, and restrictions are posted at the sites. Local fisheries officers can also provide information and closures are listed in current issues of the *B.C. Tidal Waters Sport Fishing Guide*. Restrictions must be strictly obeyed, as serious illness can occur if they are ignored.

Even more dangerous to unwary consumers of shellfish is paralytic shellfish poisoning (PSP), commonly known as red tide, a deadly phenomenon that is caused naturally by microscopic algae that proliferate in the sea under certain conditions. Fed by sunlight, a "bloom" of algae occurs when high concentrations are produced by wind and tide. Red tide is sometimes, although not always, visible as a reddish tinge to the water.

The algae only affects bivalve molluscs — that is, shellfish with two shells, such as oysters, clams and mussels — which collect the poison in their digestive glands. Although the poison does not affect the shellfish, people or other animals who consume contaminated shellfish may suffer the full effects of the poison.

Paralytic shellfish poisoning attacks the nervous system, causing muscular paralysis. The first symptom of poisoning is numbness or tingling of the lips and tongue, which may spread to the fingers and toes if untreated. This progresses to loss of muscle coordination, and eventually death by asphyxiation.

The B.C. *Sport Fishing Guide* recommends that at the first sign of poisoning, the victim should induce vomiting, take a laxative and drink a

Boats at anchor in Squitty Bay, Lasqueti Island.

solution of baking powder, then seek medical attention as quickly as possible.

The federal department of fisheries is responsible for monitoring toxicity of shellfish due to red tide, and bans shellfish collecting in affected areas. These areas sometimes remain closed for years; if you are in doubt as to whether the ban is still in effect, check with the local fisheries officer. Never take a chance and risk eating the shellfish in such areas — it is potentially fatal.

When You Arrive by Private Boat

Many of these islands are well-known to pleasure boaters; others are just beginning to be destinations as the southern anchorages become more crowded and the northern coast opens up. Cruising guides and other yachting books are available for many of the islands mentioned here.

Although this book is not a boating guide, it contains much information of interest to boaters: government wharves, safe anchorages and nearby shoreline activities.

All boaters should be knowledgeable about tides, currents and weather conditions and carry proper sounding gear, hydrographic charts and tide and current tables. This book does not detail locations of reefs and rocks or other hazards, or other information normally carried by pleasure boaters.

The Metric System

This book conforms to the metric system, with the exception of the boating sections, which use nautical miles for paddling distances (conforming to current standards used on hydrographic charts).

The metric system can sometimes be confusing for those not used to it. The following charts are designed to provide simple multiplication factors for conversion of metric to imperial equivalents.

TO CHANGE	TO	MULTIPLY BY
centimetres	inches	.4
metres	feet	3.3
kilometres	miles	.63
square metres	square yards	1.25
square kilometres	square miles	.4
hectares	acres	2.5
kilograms	pounds	2.2

TO CHANGE	TO	MULTIPLY BY	
inches	centimetres	2.5
feet	metres	.3
miles	kilometres	1.6
square yards	square metres	.8
square miles	square kilometres	2.6
acres	hectares	.4
pounds	kilograms	.45

FAHRENHEIT/CELSIUS SCALE

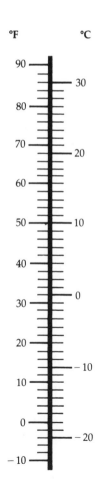

°F °C

Gabriola Island

Sandstone Galleries and Beaches

 Gabriola is a kidney-shaped island of 50 square kilometres

lying 5.5 kilometres east of Nanaimo on Vancouver Island.

Often overlooked by tourists, it is a quiet, friendly island with a pleasantly

lived-in atmosphere. Numerous beach accesses lead to diverse shorelines,

from sandstone ledges to sandy bays and long, exposed shores with pebble

beaches.

The north and south shores of Gabriola are fairly smooth, with few

indentations; at the northwest and southeast ends of the island are several

bays and small offshore islands. Gabriola is well-known to boaters, as two

channels around the island — Gabriola Passage, between Gabriola and

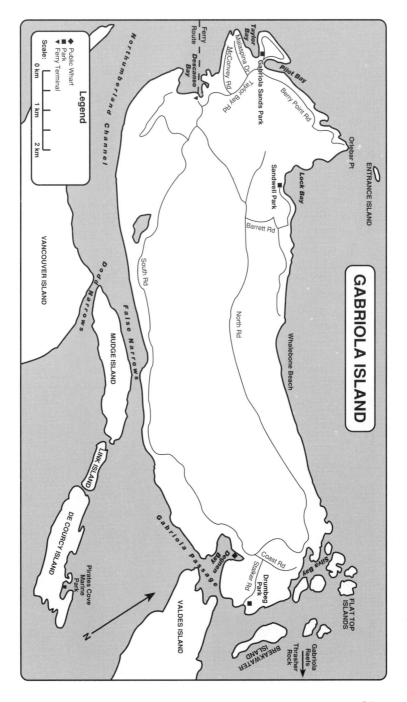

GABRIOLA ISLAND

Legend

◆ Public Wharf
■ Park
▼ Ferry Terminal

Scale:
0 km
1 km
2 km

Northumberland Channel

VANCOUVER ISLAND

Ferry Route

Taylor Bay

Descanso Bay

Malaspina Dr

McConvey Rd

Taylor Bay Rd

Gabriola Sands Park

Pilot Bay

Berry Point Rd

Orlebar Pt

ENTRANCE ISLAND

Sandwell Park

Lock Bay

Barrett Rd

South Rd

North Rd

Whalebone Beach

Dodd Narrows

False Narrows

MUDGE ISLAND

LINK ISLAND

DE COURCY ISLAND

Pirates Cove Marine Park

Gabriola Passage

Degnen Bay

Coast Rd

Stalker Rd

Drumbeg Park

Silva Bay

FLAT TOP ISLANDS

BREAKWATER ISLAND

Gabriola Reefs

Thrasher Rock

VALDES ISLAND

N

31

Valdes islands, and Dodd Narrows, between Mudge and Vancouver Island — are some of the busiest in the Gulf Islands. They are the most-used entrances from the north to the sheltered waters of the southern Gulf Islands group. Silva Bay, just north of Gabriola Passage, has a number of marinas and is one of the most popular anchorages in the Gulf Islands, as well as being a centre of island life.

Mainly a residential island, Gabriola became the centre of controversy in the 1970s when large tracts of land were subdivided into 2,000-square-metre lots. Domestic water and septic disposal have traditionally been problematic on the dry, rocky Gulf Islands, and public concerns were raised about the ability of the island's limited resources to support the potential population if Gabriola was further subdivided. In 1974, the Islands Trust was established by the provincial government to pass bylaws regulating development on the islands. For Gabriola, the Islands Trust was formed just in time to prevent what might have been drastic overdevelopment.

Today some 2,500 permanent residents make Gabriola their home, a population that swells significantly in the summer with visitors and cottagers. The population is concentrated to the north and south of the island and a friendly rivalry exists between north and south islanders — perhaps dating from pioneer days, when a visit to the other end of the island meant a good part of the day in a horse and buggy or rowboat. Many islanders commute to work on Vancouver Island; others are involved in service industries on Gabriola. Like many Gulf Islands, there is a high

Silva Bay marina.

32

proportion of retired people and a thriving cottage industry in pottery and other arts and crafts — evidenced by signs at gateposts around the island and at local craft outlets.

Gabriola is an appealing island, with fine beaches and bays and just enough island politics to make life interesting. For years the island has been involved in the Great Bridge Debate. Sometimes the issue lies dormant, but it always resurfaces — often at election time. The proposal would construct a terminal for ferries from the mainland on Gabriola (replacing the terminal at Nanaimo), with bridges linking Gabriola, Mudge and Vancouver Island. The combined bridge and ferry system would relieve the overburdened system between Vancouver Island and the mainland, shaving significant time from the crossing. Residents for the most part want to retain their home as an island, but competing bumper stickers show there are mixed views on the issue: "Real islands don't have bridges," and "Bridges don't have lineups."

Getting There

Descanso Bay is the Gabriola terminus for ferries from downtown Nanaimo; schedules are available on B.C. Ferries, or at the Infocentre in Nanaimo. Check telephone directories or inquire at local outlets for information on air transportation and water taxis to the island, and taxis and bicycle rentals on Gabriola.

A Route to Follow

Gabriola has no "downtown" area; scattered stores, pubs and marinas service residents and visitors. From the ferry terminal at Descanso Bay, one main road circles the island, its name changing from South Road to North Road at Silva Bay. Another major artery, Taylor Bay Road, leads to residential and recreational areas at the northern end of the island.

To take the main route, continue straight along South Road after disembarking from the ferry at Descanso Bay. Keep to the right at the junction with North Road, where there is a cluster of stores, a gas station, a post office and an old community hall. It is about 14 kilometres from here to Silva Bay.

After passing the golf and country club, the road winds through a forest of large second-growth firs interspersed with arbutus. Glimpses of False Narrows and Mudge Island can be caught through the trees as the road descends a long hill to Brickyard Beach. There is a parking area just off the road, with picnic tables, where you can stop to admire the view of Mudge Island across False Narrows. The beach was once the site of a brickyard that operated here from the early part of the century to the Depression, making bricks of the red island clay. Broken shards of bricks are still visible among the beach pebbles. At low tide, there are often people digging clams here. The tidal current runs through False Narrows at 4 or 5 knots; ripples and eddies are clearly visible from the shore.

The road follows the coastline for several kilometres, past homes fronting on the scenic passage between Gabriola and Mudge islands. At Stokes Road, there is a parking area beside the cemetery and a path to a beach overlooking the shallows of False Narrows. In spring, huge numbers of gulls, eagles, seals and sea lions gather in this passage. Many great blue herons frequent the tidal flats — it's not unusual to see 25 at one time. The herons are year-round residents, feeding in the narrows and nesting in a nearby heronry.

The cemetery has fallen into disrepair, but the graves here bear many of the names seen on roads and bays around Gabriola — Silva, Degnen, Hughes, Easthom — with dates going back to the 1880s. Some of the headstones, such as that of Thomas Martin, aged 23, killed in a mine explosion in Nanaimo, May 3, 1887, are poignant reminders of early hardships on the coast.

After skirting Degnen Bay, a protected anchorage with a government wharf and boat launch, the road moves inland. At Stalker Road, there is

Old log church near Silva Bay.

a turnoff to Drumbeg Park, one of three provincial parks on the island. The next point of interest on the main road is Silva Bay, a scenic area where rocky, moss-covered headlands overlook a deeply indented bay protected by the Flat Top Islands. Marinas here service both visiting boaters and the local community, with laundry facilities, pub, restaurant, diving shop, shipyards, accommodation and a variety of retail stores. Unfortunately, these private marinas offer the only access to the beach and the water.

As the road swings into Silva Bay, there is a small log church on the left side of the road, built in 1912 on land donated by pioneer John Silva. The church is still in service as St. Martin's Church of the Anglican/Catholic Eucharist.

Near Silva Bay, South Road becomes North Road as it loops around to return to Descanso Bay. The road moves inland, passing through tall, second-growth forest, where overarching branches enclose the road. It is particularly lovely in summer, when sunlight filters through the leaves and dapples the road.

About 9 kilometres from Silva Bay, Barrett Road leads off to the right, giving access to residential areas around Whalebone Beach and Sandwell Provincial Park. These beaches, on the exposed north shore of the island, look directly across the broad expanse of Georgia Strait to the distant mountains of the mainland.

After Barrett Road, North Road continues past a small shopping area before rejoining South Road. At this junction, bear right onto South Road; just before the ferry terminal, turn right again onto Taylor Bay Road, the main artery for the populated northern tip of the island.

Some 2 kilometres from the junction there is a small shopping centre which caters to various needs of islanders and visitors. A short jaunt to the left is the parking area for Gabriola Sands Provincial Park, known more descriptively as Twin Beaches. The park comprises two beaches, one adjacent to the parking lot, the other across a wide grassy field; there are pit toilets and picnic tables, and drinking water from a hand-operated pump.

The north-facing beach of Pilot Bay looks out to the open ocean and is exposed to brisk northeasterly breezes, but there are interesting rock formations to hike along; the beach of Taylor Bay is larger, warmer and faces Vancouver Island. Both beaches have fine sand and plenty of driftwood for backrests, and they're safe for children as the slope is quite gradual.

The cottages by Twin Beaches have a settled-in look — the quintessential beach community. The sandy neck of Twin Beaches widens into Tinson Point, an area of beachfront homes along rocky shorelines. To explore the peninsula, take De Courcy Drive. It circles the area and provides several accesses to the beach. Watch for narrow overgrown paths that lead between properties; they are marked with concrete markers incised with "Beach Access," but are often overgrown or overturned. The perimeter of Tinson Point is composed of sandstone slabs and fingers jutting into the ocean.

Return to the main road and turn left. The road skirts the coast, revealing glimpses of seaside homes, wind and wave-battered foreshore, and ferries passing between the mainland and Nanaimo. A sign for Berry Point Road marks a left turn just before a steep hill. Follow Berry Point Road to its end near Orlebar Point (also known as Berry Point and Stupich's Point), where there is a small parking area and some picnic tables. There are several parking areas along the road, which is all seafront. A children's summer camp has operated here for many years: drivers should watch for large groups of youngsters along the road from Twin Beaches.

The 1-kilometre-long shoreline of Berry Point Road is a great place to spot eagles, explore tide pools, or watch the sun set behind Vancouver Island. Wind and wave-sculpted rock assumes an interesting variety of shapes; some seem to fit the human shape exactly and are very comfortable when warmed by the sun. Marine traffic is brisk here, with tugs pulling barges, ferries to the mainland and boats of all sizes. True to its name, blackberry bushes along the road bear sweet dark fruit in August.

Entrance Island lies off Orlebar Point, a bare sandstone rock crowned with the brisk red and white lighthouse buildings. Built in 1875, the Entrance Island lighthouse was the third to be erected in Georgia Strait. With thousands of tonnes of coal being shipped annually out of Departure Bay, the lighthouse was needed to guide marine traffic. While the light has saved a lot of lives, it has also claimed a few, especially in the early days, when lighthouse keepers rowed across from Gabriola in high seas to tend the light.

Berry Point Road continues around the point, but there is no public access past this point. Honey, free-range eggs, and pesticide-free apples may be available from an orchard just around the point. Return to the main road; north of here the paved road ends and the small residential subdivisions of the northern island are served by a network of gravel roads. Retrace the route to the junction with South Road, near the ferry.

If you're waiting in the ferry lineup and want to stretch your legs, you can walk about 400 metres up South Road, to where a short trail leads to a sandstone shelf in the forest, where there are perfectly round holes of varying depths. This is the site of a millstone quarry that operated briefly on Gabriola.

As far back as the 1850s Newcastle sandstone was known to be of superior quality and it was natural to explore nearby Gabriola for its potential. By 1889, a quarry to remove building blocks was operating near Descanso Bay. Several years after the quarry had ceased operation, it was reopened as a pulpstone quarry, taking out the huge 1- to 2-tonne stones used to grind raw logs into pulp in the paper-making process. By 1932 the quarry was in full production, but the initial promise shown by the Gabriola sandstone did not materialize. It was found to have flaws in the form of concretions, often embedded in the stone and not visible until it was worn down, and mica, which caused the pulp to tear. A further development, the introduction of synthetic stones, sealed the issue, and the quarry ceased production entirely by 1936. Now filled with water, the holes at the sight in the forest are home to a variety of aquatic life. Some of the reject stones can be seen at the gateway of a home along South Road.

What the Main Route Misses

A number of short jaunts off the main road will take you to some of the other points of interest around Gabriola.

Spring Beach Drive Beach Access

This is a pretty, sand and fine gravel beach with tumbled driftwood and Garry oaks overhanging the water. From here, there are views of the cliffs of Valdes Island, Pirates Cove Marine Park directly across on De Courcy Island, and Link and Mudge islands.

To get to it turn off South Road onto Price Road, then right onto Island View Drive. Continue to Grilse Road and turn left, then right onto Spring Beach Drive. Go to the end where there is a parking area. A short trail lined with chest-high horsetails leads to the beach, which can be explored for some distance in either direction. There are quite a few waterfront homes along the low bluff overlooking the water, many with steep stairways to the beach.

Degnen Bay

Degnen Bay, a deep indentation on Gabriola's south shore, is a protected harbour with a government wharf. To get to the bay, turn onto Degnen Bay Road from South Road. The road runs along the water and leads to the government wharf at the end of the bay. The island visible at the mouth of the bay is Indian reserve.

A petroglyph is carved on a sandstone slab at the end of Degnen Bay. It was first discovered in 1874 by a government surveyor, who used it as a marker for a surveying line. The carving is probably of a killer whale, with the dorsal fin and flukes, although the nose is a porpoise shape.

Degnen Bay is named for one of Gabriola's pioneers, Thomas Degnen, who preempted 65 hectares here in 1862, which he developed into a thriving farm. Gabriola farms enjoyed great success, becoming suppliers to the developing coal town of Nanaimo. Degnen bought a large steam launch to transport produce from Gabriola farms to market in Nanaimo; eventually the farms were so successful that a scow was towed alongside.

Drumbeg Provincial Park

A provincial park sign on South Road notes that the turnoff for Drumbeg Park is 400 metres ahead, but it is easy to miss the turn, as the actual road is not marked. After the sign, watch for Coast Road and turn right. Turn right again at Stalker Road and drive for nearly a kilometre. Watch carefully for a small green provincial park sign posted high on a tree and turn left. The parking lot is a short drive down this dirt track.

Drumbeg Park was established in 1971, and named for the Scottish home of a former owner, Neil Stalker. Pit toilets, picnic tables and an information shelter are the only facilities in this 20-hectare park. The small sandy beach is enclosed by smooth sandstone ledges that form the arms of the bay. The ledges invite sunbathers and trap large pools of water, perfect for toddlers to splash in.

Trails lead to left and right from the parking lot. To the left, a perimeter path leads through beautiful Garry oaks and Douglas firs to a grassy bluff which overlooks Breakwater, Kendrick and Valdes islands. Broom has taken over the meadow and bluffs and the area is a mass of yellow in the spring.

Shoreline Garry oak north of Drumbeg Provincial Park.

To the right, the trail leads through a semiopen forest where boats can be seen navigating Gabriola Passage. The tide can rip through Gabriola Passage at 8 knots and a white line of foam is visible at times. There are extensive shell middens all around the park, which was the historical territory of the Coast Salish Indians.

The shoreline trail can be hiked in an hour or so, but there is no reason to hurry in this beautiful small park, where you can watch the tide change and spot eagles soaring overhead. Side trails lead back through the forest and grasslands, where the foundations of old buildings are still visible. Those who want a longer walk can continue north from the park, hiking the beach almost all the way to Silva Bay. Steep dropoffs along the shore prevent hikers from getting past the entrance to the bay across from the Flat Top Islands. It takes about two hours to hike there and back.

Along the shore, the sandstone is pockmarked with perfectly round holes. The holes are probably places where concretions — spherical masses that form around a nucleus of organic matter, such as a leaf, shell or piece of bone — have weathered out. They are usually harder than the surrounding sandstone, but the area immediately around the concretion tends to weather, and eventually it pops out. The holes can vary in size from a centimetre to over a metre.

Whalebone Beach

Whalebone Beach is a long shallow scoop in the northern coastline of the island. Exposed to the open expanse of Georgia Strait, with no offlying islands for protection, there is an almost bleak sense of solitude here that has its own unique charm.

To get to the beach, turn onto Barrett Road from North Road and drive for about 2 kilometres. Turn right onto Whalebone Drive and continue to the end of the road, about 1.5 kilometres, where there is a parking area. A short path leads to the water through a pleasant shady forest of alder and fir, with an understory of ferns and salal.

The narrow sandy beach extends for several hundred metres, then changes to large round stones with conglomerate outcroppings at the low tide line. About 200 metres to the left of where the path joins the beach, there is a group of rocky islets offshore where seals haul out, sharing the rocks with gulls and cormorants. In winter and spring they are joined by sea lions. At a low tide they can be seen at fairly close quarters.

The shoreline is lined with private homes, but the beach is seldom crowded and often deserted; it is a great place for a solitary walk with only the gulls and seals for company.

Sandwell Provincial Park

Created in 1988, Sandwell encompasses 12 hectares at Lock Bay, on the north side of the island. To get to the park, turn off North Road onto Barrett Road. Turn left at Bluewater, then left onto the Strand and follow it to the end, where there is a signposted parking area. The path, about 1 kilometre long, follows along a ledge with a sharp drop to the beach and a steep, perhaps 30-metre cliff to the other side. Jumbled sandstone slabs are piled against the cliff, seemingly held in place by the roots of large Douglas firs, maples, arbutus and the tangled undergrowth. At the end the path dips steeply to the beach. The beach is composed of large round pebbles and rocks with sandy pockets. Wildflowers — wild roses, beach pea, and clover — grow profusely on the grassy banks in spring and early summer. The mountains of the mainland form the backdrop for ferries passing between Vancouver Island and Horseshoe Bay, and the lighthouse at Entrance Island is visible to the west.

A number of petroglyphs have been carved into sandstone boulders near the high tide line at Lock Bay. Some are heavily eroded; one is more deeply incised. The area was reportedly used for ceremonial purposes by Coast Salish natives.

McConvey Road Beach Access

There are many beach accesses around Gabriola, a pleasant way to see the varying coastline and viewpoints. This particular access is directly across the small, shallow cove from Malaspina Galleries. The point is formed of broad sandstone benches and smooth rounded boulders; around the point are more beautiful sandstone formations. Although they are not as large as the galleries, there are a variety of shapes, with caves, boulders and perfectly round holes bored through rock walls.

To get to the beach access, turn onto McConvey Road from Taylor Bay Road. Continue to the end where there is a parking area. A small concrete marker and overgrown path mark the access.

Malaspina Galleries

The Malaspina Galleries are always mentioned in connection with Gabriola and are considered one of the island's main attractions. This might not seem warranted to visitors today, as the formation is significantly eroded and defaced with graffiti. Nevertheless, the galleries have a fascinating history, and underneath the spray paint, they are still a remarkable natural phenomenon.

The galleries are formed of a sandstone cliff that has been eroded by wind and wave action to resemble a large curved wave about to break. The sculpted shape of this particular formation is due to the lack of joints and fractures, and to its orientation to the main storm waves.

You can walk the length of the galleries, about 100 metres, on a wide ledge underneath the curve of the cresting wave about 4 metres overhead. The weathering process is fairly rapid in geological terms. Graffiti of a few years ago can be seen as raised letters on the stone — where the paint has protected it from erosion. In a few more years, these too will have disappeared and the next generation of graffiti will have taken its place. The ledge is now only a couple metres wide in places. Some day it will no longer be possible to walk beneath the cliff.

The fame of the galleries dates back to Spanish exploration in the 18th century. In 1792 Galiano and Valdes anchored in the tiny cove here and they were sufficiently impressed by the sandstone formations that a sketch of them accompanied the reports of their voyage.

Locals dive from the ledge at high tide or sunbathe on the grassy point of land above the galleries, which is a regional park. The moss and grass-covered point is very pleasant; a path leads through sparse, wind-stunted arbutus to the galleries, and long, flat sandstone formations form the shoreline on the other side of the point.

To get to the galleries, turn onto Malaspina Drive from Taylor Bay Road. Park at the end of the road and follow the trail to the point.

Emergencies and Information

There is an RCMP detachment on Gabriola Island. The nearest hospital is in Nanaimo and the island has its own medical clinic; phone numbers

Malaspina Galleries.

and hours are posted. Emergency numbers are listed at the front of the telephone directory, or the operator may be able to help.

Information on facilities and services on the island is available at the Infocentre in Nanaimo, or from businesses and marinas. The local paper, *The Flying Shingle* (named for the islanders pet name for the former ferry), is a good source of information about events and services on the island.

Camping and Accommodation

There is no provincial campground on Gabriola, but limited private campsites are usually available at resorts at Silva Bay and elsewhere on the island. There are several bed and breakfast establishments, inns and lodges. For current listings, check the local chamber of commerce or Tourism B.C.'s annual *Accommodations* booklet, described in Chapter One.

Shopping and Services

Marinas at Silva Bay and two main shopping areas, on Taylor Bay Road near Gabriola Sands Park, and on North Road near the junction with South Road, provide islanders with a variety of services. Real estate offices, post office, bakeries, grocery stores, video rentals, bookstores, a liquor store, craft outlets and other amenities can be found here. Locals can provide information on pubs, restaurants, marinas and other services.

Many Gabriola artisans sell from home studios as well as retail outlets; check for signs around the island.

Recreation and Events

Gabriola has a nine-hole golf course and tennis courts on North Road. Check with local outlets for information on renting bicycles, kayaks, canoes or boats, or for details on diving, horseback riding, and fishing and cruising charters. An annual Salmon Barbecue is held in August at the Community Hall on South Road.

Hiking — Backroads and Beaches

Public hiking trails on Gabriola are limited, but a good system of beach accesses allow hiking along the foreshore. Sandwell and Drumbeg provincial parks offer pleasant, easy walking in beach and forest environments (see What the Main Route Misses for descriptions of the parks). Gabriola roads, particularly Berry Point Road, can also provide pleasant hiking with beautiful beach views.

Paddling and Small Boating
— Strong Tides and History

Because of the rapid tidal streams around Gabriola Passage, False Narrows and Dodd Narrows, paddlers wanting to explore some of Gabriola's interesting coastline and surroundings should have copies of tide and current tables and know how to use them.

False Narrows and Mudge Island

Distance: variable. *Launching*: El Verano Drive.

From here you can explore the south shoreline of Gabriola and get across to Mudge Island. Dozens of small aluminum cartoppers are usually parked here by Mudge Island residents who commute across False Narrows. Sometimes there are hundreds of seals, eagles and herons in the channel. The tide runs through here at up to 4 or 5 knots at spring tides, so it's best to cross at slack tide.

Pirates Cove Provincial Marine Park

Distance: 3 nautical miles. *Launching*: El Verano Drive.

Once across False Narrows, you can skirt the shoreline of Mudge, Link and De Courcy islands all the way to Pirate's Cove Marine Park on De Courcy Island. The 31-hectare park was established in 1968. Sandstone beaches and caves with cliffs offer plenty of chances for exploration. There are twelve walk-in campsites, pit toilets, picnic tables, drinking water and 4 kilometres of hiking trails. It is a lovely sheltered anchorage, but it can be extremely crowded in summer, when boats often raft together, and you wouldn't want to swim in the water of the cove.

De Courcy Island has a rather lurid past as the site of a quasi-religious organization set up by one of B.C.'s most colourful figures. Brother XII, born Edward Arthur Wilson and self-named as the twelfth greatest mind of all time, remains shrouded in mystery to this day. There are various versions of the Brother XII story, and the debate as to whether he was a mystic or a con man will probably never be completely resolved.

Having left his clerk's job in Victoria to travel the world and study eastern religions and mysticism, Edward Wilson ended up in England, where he laid the foundations of the future Aquarian Foundation and adopted the name Brother XII. In 1927 he returned to British Columbia, following a vision of a mysterious place surrounded by the sea and shrouded in massive cedars, and began gathering a group around him. They settled, appropriately enough, in Cedar, near Nanaimo. Over the ensuing years, more people — many of them wealthy and some highly educated and literate — were attracted to the colony. Although his motives for collecting it may be debated, some historians believe that a great deal of money passed through Brother XII's hands. It's said that all money not spent on immediate needs was transferred to gold and small bills.

Despite some unrest among the followers, some of whom were having difficulty accepting Brother XII's relationships with women in the group, plans were made to purchase land on Valdes and De Courcy islands. The islands were perfectly situated to keep outsiders away from the colony.

Brother XII's leadership was undermined when Myrtle Baumgartner, his chosen partner whom he had dubbed Isis to his Osiris, gave birth to a baby girl. The upcoming birth had been built up as the reincarnation of the Egyptian god Horus, who would become a Christ-figure in 1975, and it was immediately obvious to everyone that the infant girl could not fill the role. Brother XII reportedly flew into a rage, blaming the doubters for the mix-up. Mrs. Baumgartner, confused and depressed, left the settlement and eventually became insane.

Disagreements among members of the colony ended up in Nanaimo courts in 1928, with charges and countercharges being laid by Brother XII and the Foundation's secretary-treasurer, Robert England. Mary Connally, an elderly woman who is reputed to have given her entire fortune to Brother XII, testified that she had donated sums to him personally, not to the registered foundation, and that is why it did not show on the books. When the dust settled, Robert England had disappeared, Brother XII had been cleared, but the Foundation was in disarray.

After the Isis incident, Brother XII chose as his consort the infamous Madam Zee. Despite the secrecy surrounding the community, strange stories seeped to the outside world, stories that men and women were separated and obliged to occupy opposite ends of the island, that Brother XII held court at the female end, that Madam Zee was a sadist who brutalized helpless members of the colony.

As the years went on, the colony became more and more defended. Rifles and handguns were ordered and fortifications built, with structures to mount the guns. Detachments of men were detailed to patrol the island and signs were erected warning visitors to keep off. Then Mary Connally had a change of heart and went to the police, saying she wanted her money back. By 1933, when the courts had judged that Brother XII should recompense Mary Connally, he and Madam Zee had disappeared, preceded by a flurry of activity when "dozens" of heavy wooden boxes, supposedly carefully counted and recounted by Brother XII, had been loaded onto his yacht, the *Lady Royal*. What was thought to be the remains of the boat were later found dynamited, but despite searches of all ports, Brother XII and Madam Zee — and the boxes — were never found.

Even though Brother XII is long-gone, his life is still immersed in controversy. History-writers continue to offer significantly different interpretations of the facts. Whether the group at Cedar and De Courcy Island was enslaved by an evil cult figure or whether it was an attempt at a philosophical and spiritual community that fell victim to human failings will likely never be known.

The remains of the colony could be seen at the south end of the island for many years, but the land is privately owned.

Flat Top Islands

Distance: variable. *Launching*: Silva Bay.

The Flat Top Islands are an interesting area to explore by small boat, and the inside shores are quite protected. The islands are all privately owned, but you can beach a small craft on the foreshore below the high tide line. The islands are extremely dry, and one of them is still recovering from a fire several years ago, so be careful.

Lock Bay and Whalebone Beach

Distance: 3 nautical miles, round trip. *Launching*: Berry Point Road.

This is an easy paddle around Orlebar Point, but watch for strong winds that rise in the afternoon. Leboeuf is a pretty bay with a small island just offshore. Sandwell Provincial Park is located at Lock Bay, where there are petroglyphs and a hike through the woods.

Silva Bay, with the Flat Top Islands in the background.

45

When You Arrive by Private Boat

Silva Bay

Silva Bay is a completely protected anchorage sheltered by the offlying Flat Top Islands. There is ample anchorage in the bay and private marinas offer a complete array of facilities. The Flat Top Islands make a good destination for an exploration by dinghy.

The entrance to the bay can be tricky. A beacon between Vance and Tugboat islands marks an underwater reef that has been the bane of many boaters, who are often thankful for the shipyard at Silva Bay. So many people have fetched up on the reef that it has been dubbed "Bread and Butter Rock" by local wags.

Degnen Bay

This is a pretty bay with protected anchorage in the northeast arm and a government wharf where you can tie up. There is a petroglyph just

The Spirit of Chemainus *on the ways at Silva Bay.*

above low tide at the head of the bay. The island in the mouth of the bay and a small area on the southwest point are Indian reserve. Silva Bay, with shops and other facilities is about 2 kilometres away by road. Drumbeg Park is just around the corner, less than 2 kilometres to the southeast.

Drumbeg Park

Temporary anchorage is available here for small boats. The park is a great place to swim, explore, fish or scuba dive. The park has a fine sand beach, forest trails, pit toilets and picnic tables (see What the Main Route Misses for details on the park).

Percy Anchorage

There is a small government wharf on the south side of Gabriola. Log booms frequently line the shore east of here, and small boom boats are often moored at the wharf. Just north of the wharf, temporary anchorage is available at Percy Anchorage, but it is subject to frequent westerlies. Boaters often wait here for favourable tides in Dodd Narrows.

Descanso Bay

Spanish explorers Galiano and Valdes named this bay Cala del Descanso, which means "small bay of rest." It is unprotected from northwest winds, but a good refuge in a southeaster. The ferry terminal for Nanaimo is at the head of the bay, and stores, a post office and the local library are located within a short walk.

Taylor Bay

This is a good temporary daytime anchorage, a place to enjoy swimming at a safe sandy beach and walking along the sandstone foreshore to the Malaspina Galleries. Grocery, gift, liquor and hardware stores are just a short stroll from the beach. Frequent night-time westerlies blow across from Vancouver Island, making it unsafe for overnight anchoring.

Pilot Bay

Directly across from Taylor Bay, Pilot Bay has access to all the same amenities, but provides more protection from all but northeast winds. Apparently, pilot boats which guided ships into Nanaimo Harbour once anchored here.

Gabriola Fishing

Gabriola Reefs

Launching: Silva Bay.

Gabriola Reefs, just outside the Flat Top Islands, provide excellent opportunities to find ling and rock cod. Coho and chinook are good here from April to September. Fish from the dropoff at the outside of Grant Reef to Gabriola Reef and Thrasher Rock.

Orlebar Point

Launching: Berry Point Road.

Locals jig for bottomfish along the coastline from Orlebar Point to Descanso Bay. Coho and chinooks congregate around a hole off Orlebar Point, especially in July. The ledge on the outside of Entrance Island is also good.

Northumberland Channel

Launching: The end of El Verano Road or government wharf on Wharf Road.

Northumberland Channel and Dodd Narrows are prime areas to troll for chinook and coho, as the bottom is free of reefs. Fish from Percy Anchorage to Descanso Bay along the Gabriola coastline. Dodd Narrows should be attempted only with a powerful boat as tides can be treacherous.

Gabriola Scuba Diving

Gabriola has long been a destination for scuba divers. There are air stations and other facilities on the island.

Gabriola Passage

Boat dive: Launching at Degnen or Silva Bay.

This dive is for experienced divers only, and should be made at slack tide, as the tidal currents run up to 8 knots. Other hazards include frequent marine traffic, the most dangerous to divers being log booms that are towed through the pass. Always surface close to shore.

The rewards are well worth it, though, as the rapid currents promote the growth of a vivid array of marine life. Giant boulders on the ocean floor are covered with sponges and anemones, and sailfin sculpins are frequently sighted. Diving is best between Josef and Cordero points, with the most interesting areas being the sides of the channel to about 18 to 21 metres.

Off Cordero Point there are two or three sandstone caves, which harbour wolf-eels. Octopi can be found in the crevices. Josef Point is rockier, with more boulders. Life is more diverse on this side, with sculpins, decorated warbonnets, sea squirts and rock scallops. Some areas are carpeted with tunicates. Swimming scallops are found in the shallows and tidal areas, away from the most turbulent current. Giant barnacles litter the ocean floor. Look in the empty casings for the life hiding inside: sculpins, warbonnets and baby octopi.

Breakwater Island

Boat dive: Launching at Silva or Degnen Bay.

This area is known for its abundance of wolf-eels, which can be found at the south tip in great numbers. It is a good dive because shelter is always available in the lee of the island, regardless of wind direction. Divers can go in on the east side in most conditions.

Flat Top Islands

Boat Dive: Launching at Silva Bay.

The advantage of the Flat Top Islands is that you can dive almost any time, as the inner passages are very protected. The area surrounding Carlos Island and the wall extending west along Gabriola's north shore, which drops off from a 15-metre shelf to depths of 70 metres and more, is less protected but has an abundance of marine life. The overhangs and underwater cliffs have lots of zoanthids and scallops. Sea lions frequent the large kelp beds on the outside of the islands.

Thrasher Rock and Gabriola Reefs

Boat dive: Launching at Silva Bay.

Thrasher Rock is named for the coal ship MV *Thrasher*, which fetched up on this rock in 1880 and went down with a full load of coal. Remnants of the ship are still visible scattered from 20 to 27 metres deep. Ling cod and copper rockfish are frequent here, along with octopi. There have been occasional sightings of six-gill sharks around the rock, but they are not as frequently seen as at Flora Islet near Hornby.

Dodd Narrows

Boat dive: Launching at Degnen Bay or El Verano Drive.

One of the most dangerous channels in the area, Dodd Narrows is to be attempted only by the experienced diver with a companion in a surface boat who knows the area. Tidal currents run to 9 knots.

The surface boat can be moored out of the current at Purvis Point on Mudge Island. Divers often enter the water just before slack tide and move with the current as it changes. This is a 30- to 45-minute dive under most conditions.

The Mudge Island side of the narrows is deeper, at 27 to 30 metres, and more colourful. Some divers argue that this is the most colourful and probably most interesting dive in the southern Gulf Islands, a prime spot for underwater photography.

There are cracks and crevices, nooks and crannies, where kelp and painted greenlings, perch, decorated warbonnets — at least a few dozen species of fish — can be seen. The walls here are totally coated with anemones in a riot of colour, some plumose, all stunted and spreading because of the strong currents. Blue-clawed lithodes, only seen in high-current areas, are found here. In mating season, November to March or April, huge ling cod males guard their nests. Divers should know that it is illegal to spear them during mating and hatching season. Check under the rocks and in crevices: red Irish lords are found everywhere among the bright purple of encrusting hydrocoral.

Aside from the current, hazards include rope, cable and fishing wire that is often carried through on the current and snagged on the rocks. Log booms use the pass; be sure to check for them before entering the water. Thick kelp beds sometimes form at both ends of the narrows.

The surface of Dodd Narrows is also interesting. There are hundreds of eagles to be seen here at times, and it is not uncommon to see 50 or more of these stately birds perched in trees near shore. In winter, as many as 1,800 Steller's and California sea lions have been known to haul out along the log booms from Dodd Narrows to Duke Point.

Newcastle Island

A Varied Past

 Newcastle Island is a welcome retreat tucked into Nanaimo's busy harbour, a 336-hectare island completely preserved as a provincial marine park. There is no vehicle traffic here — it is served by a foot-passenger-only ferry — and strolling among its giant arbutus and Douglas fir, it is easy to forget that you're just a five-minute ferry ride from one of B.C.'s largest cities. Yet Newcastle wasn't always a park and many people and enterprises have left their marks upon the island.

The land itself was responsible for much of the settlement of Newcastle in the last century. Coal, and later sandstone — in the form of millwheels and building stone, were scooped and quarried from the island.

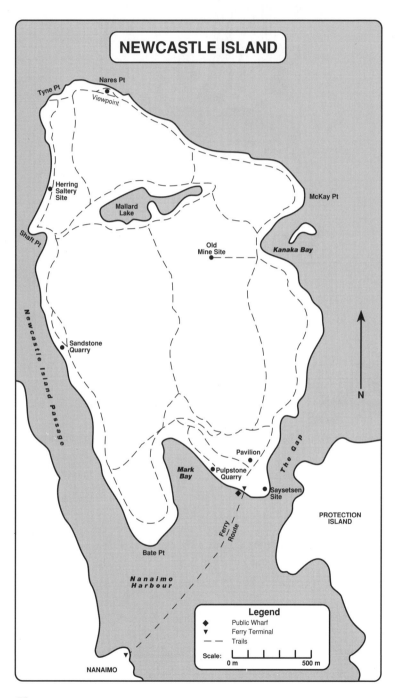

NEWCASTLE ISLAND

Nares Pt

Tyne Pt

Viewpoint

Herring
Saltery
Site

Mallard
Lake

McKay Pt

Shaft Pt

Old
Mine Site

Kanaka Bay

Newcastle Island passage

Sandstone
Quarry

N

The Gap

Pavilion

*Mark
Bay*

Pulpstone
Quarry

Saysetsen
Site

PROTECTION
ISLAND

Ferry
Route

Bate Pt

*Nanaimo
Harbour*

Legend

◆   Public Wharf
▼   Ferry Terminal
---   Trails

Scale:
0 m   500 m

NANAIMO

Later, enterprising Japanese capitalized on the riches of the sea.

But long before these waves of settlement, the island was seasonally occupied by the Coast Salish people. Newcastle Island was one stop on a cyclical journey made by the Salish each year. They came to Newcastle in January and stayed until about April. On Newcastle they harvested herring — which until the last century were said to be so thick in the bay that you couldn't row a boat across the channel between Newcastle and Vancouver Island. They then moved on to Gabriola, to collect the bulb of the camas flower. For this they waited until July, when its blue flower would distinguish the edible camas from a similar deadly variety. Then, in August, the migration continued to the mouth of the Fraser River for the sockeye and humpback salmon runs. The group returned to Vancouver Island in September, where they caught chum salmon.

This cycle went on undisturbed for centuries. Around the time Europeans began to settle the area, the villages were abandoned and Newcastle was used only as a burial ground. According to custom, bodies were placed in a sitting position in a burial box and placed in a cave, lashed to a tree or attached to a mortuary pole. Caves in the cliffs at the north and west end of the island were reportedly used for burials until at least 1890: the *Nanaimo Free Press* of 26 April, 1890, claimed in a newspaper report that boxes in the caves had bodies falling out of them.

Although the area around Newcastle and Nanaimo was explored by the Spanish in 1792, it wasn't until the 1850s that much interest was taken by Europeans. The discovery of rich seams of coal, essential to industrial expansion in the new world, ended Newcastle's quiet centuries as a seasonal home and initiated the first phase of European development.

In 1849, a native Indian of the Nanaimo area, Che-wech-i-kan, was in Fort Victoria having a gun repaired when he commented that in his area there was plenty of the black stuff being used to fuel the fire. In fact, lumps of it could be found lying along the beaches. Asked to provide proof, he agreed to bring some to Fort Victoria, but it wasn't until 15 months later, after the seasonal migrations had taken place, that Che-wech-i-kan arrived in Victoria — his canoe loaded with lumps of coal picked from the beaches around the Nanaimo area.

His arrival was greeted with excitement — coal was a valuable commodity and the mines already established near Port Hardy had not proved as productive as hoped. When analyzed, the Nanaimo-area coal was found to be of a good-quality bituminous grade. Sir James Douglas, chief factor for the Hudson's Bay Company in Victoria, investigated the find himself. He immediately took possession of the area, including Newcastle and nearby Protection islands, for the company.

By September 1852, the first ship left for Victoria, laden with 480 barrels of coal. The underground seams had barely been tapped; most of the load had been picked from surface seams by native labour. In 1854, the entire area, 2,507 hectares, was appropriated for 1 pound sterling per acre (.4 hectare). In that same year, the first group of miners and their families arrived from England to work the mines, naming Newcastle Island after England's famous coal town.

By the next decade, large-scale development had brought its own problems. Working conditions were appalling. The danger of deadly gas leaks was ever-present, with lackadaisical inspectors providing only a minimum of protection. For the miners, the sight of dead rats in the shafts became the signal for evacuation.

Living conditions during the 14-day shifts on Newcastle were equally bad: small shacks were crowded with men, smelly and stertorous from the coal dust in their breathing passages. During their days off, the men would rejoin their families in Nanaimo.

Finally, in 1864, there was the first of a series of strikes that would

The shoreline of Newcastle Island, with Nanaimo in the background.

plague the mining operation. Working conditions, evasion of safety regulations and the use of unskilled labour were the central issues.

Nevertheless, the operation around Nanaimo grew to be one of the largest collieries on Vancouver Island, with an output of over 500,000 tonnes in 1901. In its nearly 100 years of operation it raised 45 million tonnes of ore. By the time it ceased operation in 1939, the Nanaimo area was riddled with shafts and undersea workings. It was a virtual honeycomb of interconnecting tunnels that underlay Nanaimo Harbour, Newcastle Island, Protection Island and extended toward Gabriola. It is said that miners working under the sea knew when it was quitting time when they heard the rumble of the CPR cruise ships passing overhead.

On Newcastle Island, coal seams located in 1852 were being worked by 1860 and by 1875 a small dock was built in Midden Bay. The first shipment of Newcastle Island coal left for San Francisco that year. But when richer seams were found in Nanaimo, the mines at Newcastle were worked only sporadically until 1883. In 1898 a new shaft was sunk at Kanaka Bay, worked for a couple of years and then used as an exhaust ventilator for the underground network until 1938, when it was closed by a cave-in.

In 1869, while mining continued on Newcastle, another industry began to develop on the island. In that year a worldwide search was launched for top-quality stone for the new San Francisco mint. Six grand pillars were required to support the portico of the building. It was necessary to find a block large enough to cut the 10-metre lengths. Newcastle's sandstone was discovered to be of extraordinary quality. It was an attractive, even, white-grey colour and the joints and fractures in the rock were widely spaced, making it easy to take out large blocks that would not break into small irregular pieces either during quarrying or final shaping. The stone had a higher-than-usual number of quartz grains, making it strong and resistant to weathering. The first shipment was made in the mid-1870s.

The San Francisco mint — now a museum and heritage building — stands as a testament to the strength and durability of Newcastle stone. It has survived two major earthquakes, its pillars still intact, and the stone has showed remarkable resistance to weather and pollution erosion, despite being in the centre of a large city.

The quarry was worked until 1930 and employed up to 50 men; 1,800 tonnes of Newcastle sandstone were used in the B.C. Penitentiary. Some of the other buildings that were made with Newcastle sandstone are the Nanaimo post office and courthouse, the Bank of Montreal and British North American Bank in Vancouver, and St. John's Church and the Oddfellows Hall in Victoria.

In 1923, Newcastle sandstone gave rise to another industry: the quarrying of pulp millstones. Again, Newcastle stones were found to be of superior quality and were shipped to mills in the United States as well as Canada. The quarry was closed in 1932, and operations were moved to Gabriola Island.

In 1911, Japanese fishermen established a community on the west side of Newcastle Island, and a cannery, saltery and shipyard were eventually constructed by the industrious Japanese. The Newcastle saltery was one of the largest in B.C., the herring catch salted away in huge wooden crates and shipped overseas, mainly to the Orient. A fire in 1921 destroyed much of the settlement, which was immediately rebuilt. The cause was never established.

In the 1920s, the Japanese added a major shipbuilding and ship repair shop to their operations on Newcastle, with a large machine shop, generators for power and extensive fishing gear. The business thrived, constructing mainly herring boats, until 1941, when Japan entered the Second World War. In 1942 all Japanese were evacuated from the coastal areas and interned in camps in the interior of the province. The entire works of the Japanese on Newcastle were seized; the shops and equipment were dismantled and sold for a fraction of their worth. One of the two shipways was bought by Nanaimo Shipyards. Anything unsold was burnt to the ground, ending another chapter in Newcastle Island history.

Newcastle has been used for recreational purposes since the turn of the century, when the southern part of the island was a popular picnic site. In 1931, the Canadian Pacific Railway's purchase of the island raised its recreational potential to new heights of luxury and gaiety, a period that contrasts vividly with its somewhat grim coal-mining days.

The CPR got into the pleasure resort business after seeing the phenomenal success of the Union Steamship's Bowen Island resort and

The remains of the Japanese herring saltery.

other resorts along the coast. To compete with the Bowen Island resort, they constructed a tea house, picnic area, change houses, sports field, caretaker's house and a grand dance pavilion with a spring-loaded floor, which still stands today, completely restored. According to a brochure of the time, there were picnic tables to accommodate 3,500, bathing facilities with lockers, bathing suit and towel rentals, diving boards by the wharf, a concrete wading pool for toddlers, and an open-air checker board.

Trails were cleared around the island and a small man-made lake in the centre, which had been dammed for use with the coal mines, was developed. The CPR brought in muskrats and beavers so there would be wildlife to view. The *Charmer*, later replaced by the *Princess Victoria*, was tied to the dock and used as a floating hotel.

In its heyday, ships carrying up to 1,500 people came to the island on outings from Vancouver. Full orchestras were brought in for dances. Partygoers enjoyed luxury on a scale difficult to imagine today: full menus were served using beautiful old furniture, dishes and engraved silverware. A typical lunch menu began with fruit cocktail, followed by consommé Princess, lettuce and tomato salad, grilled chicken with fresh mushrooms, potato frissoles, jardinière of vegetables, neopolitan ices, and coffee.

With the outbreak of the Second World War, ships were no longer available for these pleasure excursions and the resort fell into disuse. In 1955 it was bought by the City of Nanaimo for $150,000 for use as a park. Due to financial difficulties in maintaining the park, it was sold to the provincial government in 1961, for $1, with the proviso that it become a provincial marine park. Mineral rights are still privately owned.

Getting There

The island can be reached by a private ferry that takes passengers and bicycles from the wharf behind the Civic Arena in downtown Nanaimo to Newcastle and nearby Protection Island. The ferry schedule varies according to the season; information and schedules can be obtained at the Infocentre in Nanaimo.

A Route to Follow

All transportation on Newcastle Island is by foot. A good trail follows the perimeter of the island, passing many of the island's historic sites, with side jaunts to other points of interest.

The obvious place to begin is at the ferry dock. The immediate area offers many clues to the history of the island. To the right as you get off the ferry, across a broad grassy area with large maple trees, is an embankment facing Protection Island. The dark earth interspersed with shells is an Indian midden, evidence of the Coast Salish village called Saysetsen that once stood here. Archaeologists have removed hundreds of artifacts made of stone, bone, shell, wood and metal from the site.

From here, cross back across the meadow to the pulpstone quarry, which from a distance resembles a rock garden. The tough Newcastle sandstone was sought after because of its straight grain and fine composition. The stones were cut from the quarry bed to a depth of 2 to 3 metres, each stone taking about three hours to cut. The cut was made using a large steel cylinder and split steel shot (the striations left by the shot are visible on the pulpstones at the site). A charge of gunpowder in the small hole in the centre was used to detach the stone, which was then lifted out by derrick. Only the perfect stones were shipped out and there was quite an art to choosing a cutting site. A close look at the large stones left at the quarry site will reveal the flaws that caused them to be rejected. Today the piles of pulpstones, the pools filled with stagnant water and the moss and ferns overgrowing the quarry scars, are a picturesque home for a huge colony of rabbits that use the crevices and crannies as shelter.

To continue, return to the main path and walk in a clockwise direction. The path closest to the water leads along Mark Bay, where there are large slab formations of sandstone along the shore. The forest is dominated by arbutus; in the summer, pale yellow leaves carpet the path. Past Bate Point the trail follows the shoreline overlooking Newcastle Passage, which is lined with marinas.

Midway to the northern tip of the island, several paths diverge. Take the lower path to get to the site of the sandstone quarry. Standing among the jumbled rock and sheer cuts of the quarry you can get a sense of the size of the blocks of sandstone quarried here. The blocks, 9 metres long and 1.2 metres in diameter, were lifted out by crane and loaded into the hold of a transport ship. The quarry has taken on an otherworldly appearance as the scars are softened by the encroaching forest.

North of here, the path splits, the right fork leading into Mallard Lake, the left leading back down to the water, to the site of the herring saltery. The easiest route is to take the right fork to the lake, which will return you to the main trail.

A trail encircles the lake and connects with the main trail on both sides. The trail into the lake leads through a semiopen forest with giant firs. The air is hushed and still and chances are good that you will see deer. The far end of the lake is a very different environment, as the path skirts a marshy area where tall grasses, water lilies and deciduous trees grow.

Back on the main trail, turn left and backtrack slightly to a path that leads down to the broad meadow where the saltery was located. You may be able to find a few concrete pilings, the only remains of the saltery, and traces of the midden dating back to when the bay was the site of an Indian village called Q'ulutzten.

From the meadow the path climbs around Nares Point. Past the point, an offshoot of the trail leads to a lookout high on the cliffs. Although they are not visible from above, there are reportedly caves in the cliffs where native dead were once buried. The view from here is magnificent. Far below, pleasure boats zip back and forth and ferries make their passage between Departure Bay and Horseshoe Bay on the mainland. In the distance are the shores of Vancouver Island, the islands and islets lying to the east and, across Georgia Strait, the mountains of the mainland.

This is approximately the midway point of the hike around the island. A little gazebo here provides a pleasant place to rest.

From here the path leads down to Kanaka Bay, where the shallows provide an opportunity to cool off with a swim. The bay was named for an unfortunate expatriate Hawaiian (native Hawaiians were dubbed Kanakas) who lived in Nanaimo. When he returned home to find his wife, child and mother-in-law in bed with a native Indian, he went berserk and murdered them all with an axe. He was eventually captured near Kanaka Bay and sentenced to hang at Gallows Point on Protection Island in 1869. As a non-white, authorities would not allow his burial in the graveyard, and as a non-Indian, he couldn't be buried in the Indian burial grounds. He was buried in an unmarked grave near the bay where he had been found hiding on Newcastle Island.

From here, the main path continues to skirt the shoreline to the end at the ferry dock. Particularly notable are huge arbutus trees that overhang

Pockmarked sandstone near Kanaka Bay.

the water. The shallow, narrow passage between Newcastle and Protection islands is known as The Gap. It was once a favourite place to gather crabs and shellfish (as evidenced by the native shell midden along the shore from here to your starting point). Shellfish in Nanaimo Harbour are now deemed unsafe and picking is banned.

The last stop is the old CPR Pavilion, which was the centrepiece of the pleasure resort established here in the 1930s. The building was refurbished in the 1980s by the Newcastle Island Pavilion Society. The original spring-loaded dance floor and many of the light fixtures were restored, a display depicting the island's natural and cultural history was installed and a snack bar established.

Emergencies and Information

In an emergency, call police in Nanaimo. Emergency numbers are listed in the front of the telephone directory, or the operator can likely help.

Check the Travel Infocentre in Nanaimo, or B.C. Parks, who are listed in the telephone directory, for information about facilities on Newcastle.

A quiet, sun-dappled trail.

Camping and Accommodation

The Newcastle Island campground has 18 sites as well as a large area set aside for group use (reservations are required). Wood, water and pit toilets are provided, as well as picnic tables and cooking shelters in the group area.

Recreation and Events

During the summer there are park naturalists on hand who give guided tours of various points of interest around the island and hold programs for children. Dances are sometimes held at the Pavilion on summer Saturday nights.

Hiking — Pedestrians Only

The island has more than 20 kilometres of hiking trails. The main ones are described in A Route to Follow.

Paddling and Small Boating — Be Your Own Ferry

It's possible to completely circumnavigate Newcastle in a few hours of paddling in protected waters. The only hazards are heavy boat traffic in Newcastle Island Passage and, around the northern tip of the island, wash from ferries passing in and out of Departure Bay. There is nowhere to pull out on the north side of the island, so pick your weather carefully.

Many people paddle across from Nanaimo. Cartop boats can be launched from the government wharf at Swy-a-lana Lagoon, behind the Civic Arena. Trailer boats can be launched at Brechin Marina near the Departure Bay ferry terminal.

When You Arrive by Private Boat

There are mooring buoys and a government wharf at Newcastle Island, but the wharf fills up early in the day. Mark Bay is a popular anchorage for boats visiting Nanaimo Harbour. A passenger-only ferry service operates seasonally to Nanaimo, where all amenities are available. It is a short haul by dinghy to docks in Nanaimo where you can tie up.

Lasqueti Island

A Rhythm of Its Own

Buffered from the world of fast cars and timetables by a 17-kilometre crossing of Georgia Strait, Lasqueti has a gentle rhythm all its own. Perhaps more than any other islanders, Lasqueti residents cherish and protect their isolation.

Lasqueti is 68 square kilometres and has only about 400 permanent residents. That number may double in the summer months with cottagers, but until recently, tourism has not played a significant part in the summer population bulge. Nevertheless, Lasqueti is a worthwhile destination — for a day trip or longer — not only for its natural beauty, which is considerable, but because it is so distant from the mainstream.

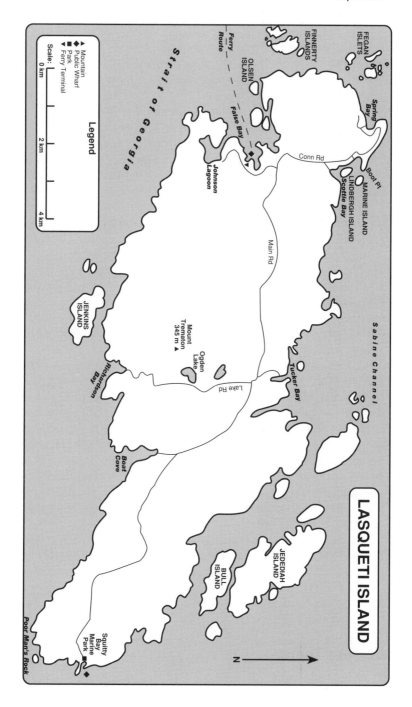

LASQUETI ISLAND

Legend

Mountain ▲
Public Wharf ◆
Park ■
Ferry Terminal ◀

Scale:
0 km   2 km   4 km

Strait of Georgia

Ferry Route

FINNERTY ISLANDS

FEGAN ISLETS

OLSEN ISLAND

Spring Bay

Boot Pt

Conn Rd

MARINE ISLAND

LINDBERGH ISLAND

Scottie Bay

False Bay

Johnson Lagoon

Main Rd

Sabine Channel

Mount Trematon 345 m ▲

Ogden Lake

JENKINS ISLAND

Lake Rd

Tucker Bay

Richardson Bay

Boat Cove

BULL ISLAND

JEDEDIAH ISLAND

Squitty Bay Marine Park

Poor Man's Rock

N

63

Island lifestyle is predicated on several — so far — immutable factors: there is no hydroelectric power on the island; all supplies must be barged in, including vehicles; there is a foot-passenger ferry service to the island; and stormy weather in the strait can isolate the island for days at a time. Visitors to the hotel, for instance, might be surprised to find they are furnished with kerosene lamps or candles — because generators are turned off at night. When all vehicles have to be barged in — at considerable expense — appearance assumes less importance; here you may see cars without doors or other nonessential paraphernalia being driven around the island roads. And without a car ferry, visitors are limited to bicycle and foot power, or to the availability of a taxi or the good nature of locals who provide transportation about the island.

Lasqueti Island is still open range, so cows and sheep amble down the roads and graze in the front yards of homes, and occasionally horses gallop wildly along in a clatter of hoofs. Feral sheep and goats, numbering in the hundreds, also wander the island. In 1875, a government report listed just two settlers on Lasqueti, each with about 200 sheep. Today's wild sheep are probably descendants of those early flocks; at the time enthusiastic estimates were made of the island being able to support up to 10,000 sheep. The feral sheep have long tails while the domestic variety are bobbed, and it is not uncommon to see wild and domestic sheep calmly grazing together inside the fenced fields.

The island has had permanent settlements since the 1870s, when land was preempted for sheep farming. The history of settlement here is typical of the boom and bust economies experienced elsewhere on the coast: dreams have come and gone, and farming, fishing, mining and logging have all played a part. Today the island is home base for a major fishing company, and limited logging still takes place, monitored closely by the community. Small cottage industries, such as crafts and a wooden button-making business, have an outlet in local shops. A small number of residents have producing farms or are employed in the few services offered on the island. Many are virtually self-sufficient, finding plenty from the land and the sea to sustain a simple lifestyle.

Perhaps most of all, Lasqueti is a marine island, bounded by the sea and the weather. If it's blowing, islanders can be marooned for several days at a time, and talk in local establishments turns to the conditions outside.

Time will change Lasqueti; this is inevitable and some will say it is long past due. But for now it remains unique, quixotic and charming for those who wish to visit there.

Getting There

A passenger ferry runs from French Creek on Vancouver Island to False Bay several times daily except Tuesday and Wednesday. For schedule information, call B.C. Ferries, or check at the dock in French Creek, or at the Parksville or Qualicum Infocentres. The 18-metre aluminum vessel was especially designed to carry small freight and passengers. Bicycles, canoes and kayaks can be carried aboard for an extra fee.

Check telephone directories or local outlets to find out about air transportation and water taxis, and for information on taxis and bicycle, canoe and kayak rentals on Lasqueti.

Some Routes to Follow

The hub of the island is False Bay, where the ferry docks. Strangers and residents all pass along the dock, under the watchful eyes of regulars who fish, run charters, or just hang out there. The first thing a visitor should do is read the notices posted on the dock: they'll list most of the information you might need to get about the island. A store, a pub and limited accommodation are located right at False Bay. A short distance up the road is a post office, a little farther on is a car repair shop, a bakery that is periodically open and a craft store. This comprises downtown Lasqueti.

Travellers are not likely to have access to a car on Lasqueti, but several day trips to interesting points on the island can be made on foot or by bicycle from False Bay. All roads on the island are gravel. The main ones are well-maintained but can be dusty when a vehicle passes. Fortunately — or perhaps unfortunately, if you've overextended your hike and you'd like to hitch a ride — traffic is infrequent. It's a good idea to pack a snack, including something to drink, as the only place refreshments are available is False Bay.

Spring Bay

This is a 6-kilometre trip each way. There is a parklike feeling to some of Lasqueti's roads, and most of this route is through tall second-growth forest. There are a few highlights to watch for along the way.

From the wharf, follow the road up the hill, passing the post office and a church hidden among the trees behind a parking lot. Near here the road passes close by an arm of False Bay known as Mud Bay (if the tide is out, the reason for its name is immediately obvious). Commercial picking of shellfish has been restricted in this bay, which is reserved for the public. At intervals you will pass a number of retail outlets and community services, including the Lasqueti car repair shop, a gift shop, a bakery that may serve delicious, old-fashioned cinnamon buns, the school and the fire hall.

A little over 1 kilometre along is the junction with Conn Road, where a magnificent heritage building is located. Completed in 1936, its identifying characteristic is the chimney, shaped like a teapot (the other chimney, a sugar bowl, is more difficult to see due to modifications). Its log-round siding is also unusual. The building was abandoned in the 1950s, but has since been faithfully restored. It has been operated as a restaurant in the summer months — reason enough for many people to make the trip to Lasqueti.

The Teapot House marks the end of Lasqueti's commercial strip. Turn left on Conn Road and continue along the road. Watch for hawks in the silvery snags at the tops of tall trees and woodpeckers flitting through the forest. Signs of habitation are sparse; infrequent driveways lead to houses hidden among the trees. Road junctions are usually marked by an array of mailboxes. Although the houses may be tucked away in the forest, the owners' personalities are revealed in the original designs of their mailboxes.

More than 3 kilometres from False Bay is Scottie Bay Road. Scottie Bay, a short jaunt down the road, is a picturesque cove protected by nearby Lindberg Island. This is a completely protected haven, and boats are often anchored in the bay. Public access to the beach is to the left of the Lasqueti Fish Company yards, which began their boatbuilding and fishing operations here in the 1950s. The wharf and float are private, although the owners may grant permission to use them.

There are interesting fossil deposits to be found along the shoreline of Scottie Bay behind Lindberg Island. A hard grey sandstone at the water line is full of broken pieces of white shell and a few nearly-complete oyster shells. These thick-walled shells almost look like they could have just

The Teapot House.

washed ashore, but they are embedded in the sandstone, which is about 85 to 88 million years old.

Returning to Spring Bay Road, continue for another half kilometre, to another road which leads to Maple Bay, a shallow bay backed with driftwood and a gravel beach. Several homes are scattered around the bay. The passage between Lindberg Island and Lasqueti dries at low tide, separating Scottie and Maple bays. An extensive shell midden is visible alongside the road to Maple Bay, evidence of habitation by a band of Coast Salish.

There is one more beach access before Spring Bay. Boot Point looks across Sabine Channel to Texada Island. Back on the main road, 1 kilometre farther, Nichols Road marks the access to Spring Bay.

Spring Bay is one of the nicest beaches around Lasqueti, with beautiful clear water and a beach of tiny, multi-coloured pebbles. In the distance are the low, wooded islands and rocky reefs of the Fegan Islets. Explorers can search out the caves in the area. The land here has all been subdivided and several homes encircle the bay, but they don't alter the beauty of the beach.

To return, retrace the route to False Bay, a round trip of 12 kilometres. The whole trip takes about two hours to walk, more depending on how much time you spend exploring or lounging about on the beaches.

Tucker Bay

Tucker Bay was once the centre of social life on Lasqueti Island. There was a good government wharf here, built in 1912, and the Union Steamship Company made Tucker Bay its weekly port of call for the next decade. Several buildings sprang up around the wharf, including a school, but by 1917 the cannery at False Bay had seduced the fickle population to the other end of the island and the school was closed. In 1923, the steamship service to Tucker Bay was drastically reduced because of dangerous reefs at the entrance to the bay, and by 1927 it was reinstituted at False Bay. When the Tucker Bay co-operative store, organized by the Farmer's Institute, burned down in 1926, and the post office was established at False Bay, the community at Tucker Bay went into decline. Today there are only private homes around the bay. Swimming and shellfish collecting are the main attractions, and from the high bluffs overlooking Tucker Bay, there are views of Texada and Jervis islands. A donkey engine there is a reminder of old logging days on the island.

To get to Tucker Bay, take the main road from False Bay, and turn right at the junction by the Teapot House. This is Main Road, which continues to Squitty Bay at the south end of the island. Continue along Main Road for about 6 kilometres, passing Pete's Lake (the water reservoir for False Bay) near the junction. You are likely to see cattle and horses along this route, as well as wildlife varying from deer to turkey vultures. There is little of note along the road, although there is an occasional old farmstead that imparts a true rural flavour.

Turn left at Tucker Bay Road and continue to the end (less than a kilometre) where there is public access. (The public access looks like it is in a private driveway, but it is public.) Old donkey engines on Tucker Bay Road are remnants of the logging of the 'twenties.

For many years there was a large stone and wood house on this road that was the scene of a commune in the 1960s and '70s. As many as 80 people were reported to belong to this loose association, and there was considerable speculation among islanders that the multitude was fed in part on sheep and cattle that did not belong to them. After construction of the big house, the property was sold and most of the group moved off the island. In 1972, two of them were charged with rustling and a two-week trial ensued, but they were never convicted. In the late '80s the big stone and wood house burned down.

Retrace the route to Main Road and go back to False Bay, or continue on to Squitty Bay. From False Bay to Tucker Bay is a total of about 8.5 kilometres, one way.

Richardson Bay

Richardson Bay is over 11 kilometres from False Bay, making a round

Ogden Lake and Mount Trematon, the highest point on Lasqueti.

trip of more than 22 kilometres, so only sturdy hikers or cyclists will find it a suitable destination.

Take the main road from False Bay, turning right onto Main Road at the Teapot House. At Lake Road, just after the Tucker Bay junction, turn right, and proceed down the narrow, twisting road, past several farms carved out of the forest. About two kilometres from Main Road is a lovely view of the steep wooded slopes of Mount Trematon across Ogden Lake. Mount Trematon, the highest point on Lasqueti at 345 metres, is named for its resemblance to an ancient turreted castle in Cornwall, England. The road here passes some huge Douglas firs, alders and maple trees. Unfortunately Mount Trematon and the lake are all privately owned, and there is no public access. Turn left at the junction to Richardson Bay Road. It is 1 kilometre from here to the bay.

One of Lasqueti's oldest and prettiest farms lies along this road. Built in 1916 and surrounded by its fruit trees planted by the original homesteaders, the house is in near-original condition. Inside the old cedar zigzag fencing, sheep graze placidly on rolling pastures.

The sharp gravel beach at Richardson Bay is suitable for swimming, but the bay isn't as scenic as some. A 201-hectare area just north of Richardson Bay was set aside as an ecological reserve in 1971. The reserve is intended to protect the unusual juniper-cactus ecosystem that thrives here, and is not a park or recreational area.

To return, retrace the route to False Bay, or go back to Main Road and continue on to Squitty Bay.

Boat Cove

Boat Cove is a little over half-way to Squitty Bay, and makes a good midway stop for cyclists or hikers to cool off with a swim. Take Main Road to the Boat Cove turnoff — 3 kilometres past the junction of Lake Road. It is then only half a kilometre to the cove. Follow the road directly to the cove. A no-trespassing sign posted on a tree is somewhat ambiguous, as it refers to the property next to the road, not to the road itself. Do not disturb the small stream here — it is a salmon-spawning stream and is stocked with fry as part of an enhancement program. Boat Cove has a good gravel swimming beach with views of Vancouver Island.

Return to Main Road and retrace the route to False Bay, or continue on to Squitty Bay.

Squitty Bay Provincial Marine Park

For years Squitty Bay has been known to recreational boaters, but it is now a destination for landlubbers as well. It is a fair distance from

False Bay: 19 kilometres, or a round trip of 38 kilometres. It's a long haul for all but the most enthusiastic hiker, but Squitty Bay has become popular amongst cyclists. There is usually someone on the island who is willing to perform taxi services.

Although the park is small, it is austerely beautiful and environmentally intriguing. The south end of Lasqueti is very different from the north, where there are forested coves and bays with sandstone and conglomerate formations typical of the more southern Gulf Islands. To the south, older volcanic rock is exposed. Severe rocky headlands, topped with bleached grass and stunted trees, are exposed to the full force of the southeast wind, which has 120 kilometres of open channel in which to gather its fury. It is also arid, and juniper and cactus thrive here in the dry subzone of the Douglas fir forest.

Squitty Bay Park comprises 13 hectares. A nature conservancy within the park is fenced to keep out deer, and feral sheep and goats, to protect the fragile desertlike ecology of this area. From a knoll in the conservancy, there are breathtaking views extending from the mainland across to Vancouver Island. On a clear day, you can see the 3,285-metre peak of Mount Baker, nearly 200 kilometres to the southeast in Washington State.

The only park facilities are pit toilets and picnic tables. No camping or fires are allowed in the park. A trail winds around the head of the bay to a low peninsula on the other side.

Squitty Bay Provincial Marine Park.

Emergencies and Information

There are no police or medical services on the island. Police matters are dealt with by the RCMP detachment in Parksville. In a medical emergency, a Canadian Coast Guard hovercraft or helicopter can be summoned from Vancouver Island.

Information on Lasqueti is available at the Infocentre in Parksville, or you can call businesses on Lasqueti.

Camping and Accommodation

There are no private or government campgrounds on Lasqueti. Limited accommodation is available in False Bay, and there may be bed and breakfast establishments on the island. Check with local directories or

Old homestead near Ogden Lake.

Tourism B.C.'s annual *Accommodations* booklet, described in Chapter One. Because of the limited accommodation, it is best to reserve ahead when planning an overnight visit to Lasqueti.

Shopping and Services

False Bay and the road leading from False Bay to Main Road have the only shopping and commercial services on the island. They include a general store, pub, overnight accommodations, post office, bakery, craft store and restaurant.

Recreation and Events

Local outlets may rent bicycles, canoes and kayaks; check at False Bay for information or for details on fishing and cruising charters. Businesses on the island can provide information on local events of interest to travellers.

Paddling and Small Boating — Islands and Bays

Probably the best way to see Lasqueti is by water. It is important to observe weather signs closely, though, as Lasqueti's exposed position in Georgia Strait makes it extremely vulnerable to winds that can blow up fast and hard.

Since there is no car ferry to Lasqueti, many paddlers explore in the vicinity of False Bay. Explorations farther afield, to the many bays and coves around Lasqueti's perimeters, should be left to experienced paddlers.

False Bay

Distance: variable. *Launching*: Wharf at False Bay.

False Bay is a large bay with an intricate coastline extended by many islands and islets. The variety of coves, inlets and islands, and the shallow waters between them, can provide hours of enjoyment just poking about at a leisurely pace. The entrance to Johnson Lagoon and many of the channels between the islands dry at low tide, so be sure to check the tide tables if you want to paddle the whole area.

The first indentation north of the ferry dock is appropriately named Mud Bay. At high tide, it is a scenic little cove, which flattens out to a wide mud bay as the tide recedes. Clams and oysters can be picked here. As you continue around the shoreline, note the large white Edwardian house close to the shore. It was barged in from Vancouver's Upper Shaughnessy district and placed with some difficulty behind a tree on the shore.

Between Higgins Island and the Lasqueti shore, watch for large openings in the embankment, old adits from early mining explorations. The earliest explorations took place well before the turn of the century, and although it was thought that Lasqueti ores held much promise, not much was ever extracted. By the 1920s, the mining operations were shut down, but there was a brief burst of activity in the 1960s. The mine shafts are on private land and should not be entered, as they can be dangerous.

Olsen (Arbutus) Island at the north entrance to the bay is appropriately named by locals for the many arbutus crowning its low rocky cliffs of volcanic basalt. Interesting homes are perched here and there on the bluffs, as well as on floats in the bay.

If time and the winds are right, you might want to extend your trip to the Finnerty Islands, another mile or so, or you may want to return to the south end of False Bay and explore Johnson Lagoon.

The completely protected waters of Johnson Lagoon have allowed a specialized ecosystem to develop. Unusually large dogfish, an abundance of jellyfish and a unique species of coral are reported to flourish in the relatively warm water of the lagoon. The shoreline is partially occupied by oyster lease. The current runs at up to 3 or 4 knots through the shallow, narrow entrance to the lagoon, so it can only be entered at high water.

Finnerty and Fegan Islands

Distance: 4 nautical miles. *Launching*: False Bay wharf.

There's about 700 metres of open water between Olsen Island and the Finnerty Islands, and the passage can be choppy. The outer edge of the Finnertys can be exposed to heavy swells and strong winds, but the inner routes are much more protected.

A paddle to the islands is a fascinating day trip from False Bay or a great overnight expedition. The islands are a recreational reserve and campers can choose among a number of tiny, perfect locations. There is no fresh water on the islands, but it's available at the wharf in False Bay. As with all wilderness camping, care should be taken to "leave nothing but footprints, take nothing but memories." This is especially true of the fragile ecosystem on the islands.

There is a magical, timeless feeling to the Finnertys, which seem so remote from civilization, so fragile, and yet so enduring. Bare, ancient rock is exposed in most places, and twisted, stunted juniper and arbutus lean away from the prevailing winds. Wherever there is a thin layer of soil, wildflowers bloom profusely in the spring. Deep spongy moss fills the crevices between rocky outcroppings, lichens leave lacy patterns on exposed rocks, and cactus nestles in the cracks. On the islands, there are no sheep and goats to destroy the delicate desert-type ecology, and it flourishes undisturbed.

At low tide, many of the channels between the islands dry, making dollars.

The Fegan Islands are another 2 miles through somewhat exposed water. They are more exposed and are lower, less wooded and rockier.

When You Arrive by Private Boat

False Bay

There is protected anchorage in the northern part of False Bay. It has interesting areas to explore and is near the only source of food and gas on the island.

The government dock has limited moorage; a portion of it is reserved for the ferry. Strong westerly winds blow up most evenings, and this part of the bay is recommended only as a temporary moorage. All the amenities you will find on Lasqueti are available within 1 kilometre of the dock: pub, restaurants, post office, and gift shop.

Richardson Bay

Locals use this cove to anchor in the summer. The bay is open to the south, but is protected from westerlies by Jenkins Island. The road leading from the head of the bay passes some pretty scenery, including one of the island's oldest farms and Ogden Lake with Mount Trematon in the background.

Boat Cove

This is another anchorage that is exposed to the south, but performs quite well in the summer. There are very few protected anchorages on this southern shore of Lasqueti, which is dominated by rugged, windswept rocks exposed to southeast gales in the winter.

Squitty Bay

Squitty Bay, at the southeast tip of Lasqueti, is a tiny slit in the rocks that affords good protection. There is a public wharf and the bay beyond the float has been dredged to provide anchorage.

For information on the shoreside attractions, see the section on Squitty Bay in Routes to Follow.

Scottie Bay

A safe anchorage in all weather, there are usually several boats anchored in Scottie Bay and it can be crowded at times with both commercial and pleasure craft. Homes are located around the bay, and the private floats and dock of a shipyards and fish company dominate the end of the bay. Supplies are available at False Bay, just 3 kilometres down the road. See Routes to Follow for more information on Scottie Bay.

Lasqueti Fishing

Sea Egg Rocks and Jenkins Island

Launching: False Bay.

There is good trolling for coho here from spring through summer, although reefs and rocks in the area can make trolling difficult. Mooching and jigging are the preferred methods. Locals fish for chinook and rockfish year-round, but the prime chinook season is April to October.

By the end of summer the main salmon runs have all tapered off. Bluebacks start in February and March and peak in May.

A peaceful rural scene near Lake Road.

Sangster Island

Launching: False Bay.

Depending on the tide, you can fish all around the reef at Sangster Island. Locals prefer to mooch at anchor here.

Poor Man's Rock and Point Young

Launching: False Bay.

Poor Man's Rock was apparently named because it was a good spot for a poor man to catch his dinner. Coho gather here from spring through summer. Try anchoring at the south end of the reef on an ebb tide.

Olsen Island to Scottie Bay

Launching: False or Scottie bays.

Troll close to the rocks in a circle around the north end of the island, from Olsen Island to past Scottie Bay, staying outside the Finnerty and Fegan islands.

Lasqueti Scuba Diving

The 17 kilometres of open water that separate Lasqueti from Vancouver Island, the lack of a car ferry, and the lack of scuba-diving facilities on the island diminish Lasqueti's appeal as a destination for divers. Snorkellers enjoy the unusual life to be found in Johnson Lagoon, and the area around Finnerty Islands.

Denman Island

An Easy Pace

 Denman is a low-profile island, 19 kilometres long and 6 kilometres wide, just a ten-minute ferry ride across Baynes Sound from Buckley Bay on Vancouver Island. Nestled against Vancouver Island and protected in the lee of Cape Lazo to the north, the climate and ocean currents around Denman are gentle — a gentleness reflected in the lifestyles of the island's 800 permanent residents. A trip to Denman is not likely to involve you in a flurry of activity. You are more likely to find yourself meandering around the island's roads, whiling away an afternoon listening to island gossip in the local cafe, or taking leisurely hikes around the parks and beaches. At night, you might steam open clams

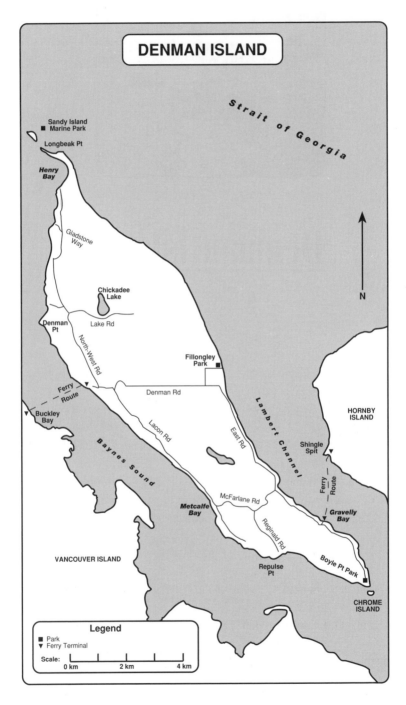

DENMAN ISLAND

Strait of Georgia

Sandy Island
■ Marine Park
Longbeak Pt

Henry Bay

N

Gladstone Way

Chickadee Lake

Denman Pt

Lake Rd

North-West Rd

Fillongley Park ■

Ferry Route

Denman Rd

Buckley Bay ▼

Baynes Sound

Lacon Rd

East Rd

Lambert Channel

HORNBY ISLAND

Shingle Spit ▼

Ferry Route

McFarlane Rd

Metcalfe Bay

Reginald Rd

Gravelly Bay ▼

VANCOUVER ISLAND

Repulse Pt

Boyle Pt Park ■

CHROME ISLAND

Legend
■ Park
▼ Ferry Terminal

Scale:
0 km   2 km   4 km

or oysters over a fire while watching the sunset fade over calm waters.

Denman was settled by fishermen and farmers in the last century. There was fine agricultural land along the east and west shores, and settlers were able to trade their surplus produce in Nanaimo and Victoria for goods they needed. Later, mining activities near Comox provided an even closer market, and the island prospered. Over the years, Denman has seen a number of small industries come and go, including a sandstone quarry and a clamshell plant at Henry Bay, where the shells lay under the surface mud to an undetermined depth. The clamshell was shipped to New Westminster, where it was used for poultry grit and fertilizer.

There is still a pervasive rural atmosphere on Denman Island. Along the main routes, turn-of-the-century farmhouses and weathered barns are surrounded by cultivated fields and orchards. More recently, residents have taken to farming the sea as well, and the west side of the island is taken up with an almost continuous string of oyster leases.

Denman is unusual for the Gulf Islands in that it has a relatively smooth coastline with no deep bays or coves. Its highest point is just 124 metres above sea level, part of a mountainous ridge that extends the length of the island. At Komass Bluffs, and at Boyle Point, steep bluffs rise from the water to a height of 80 metres, but much of the island is surrounded by gravel shoals that extend for some distance out from shore — a danger to boaters who do not know the waters.

The north end of the island is heavily wooded and sparsely settled,

The Denman Island General Store.

although residential areas are making inroads into the forest. Most of it is not publicly accessible, but old logging roads that form a network of trails throughout the area have long been used by locals for horseback riding and hiking. At the northernmost tip are Henry Bay and Longbeak Point, which are connected to Sandy Island and the Seal Islets at extremely low tides. Sandy Island has been a favourite spot for picnics and camping for many years, and in 1966 the offshore islands and islets were established as Sandy Island Provincial Marine Park. At a very low tide, the sand spit extends halfway to Goose Spit near Comox; continuing underwater, it is covered by a mere 4 metres of water. Stories are told of a time when native people walked to Denman from Comox Bay, giving rise to theories that Denman was once connected to Vancouver Island.

Before European settlement, Denman was used seasonally by Comox Indians, who occupied the area from Parksville to Comox in the thousands. Their name for Denman signified Inner Island, while Hornby was the Outer Island. Petroglyphs at Chrome Island, off Denman's south end, and middens at Henry and Metcalfe bays and near Fillongley Park testify to many years of use by these Salish people. By the turn of the century, they had stopped coming to the island.

Getting There

Denman Island is served by B.C. Ferries from Buckley Bay on Vancouver Island, a ten-minute crossing of Baynes Sound. Schedules are available from B.C. Ferries or at Infocentres on Vancouver Island. Check local listings for information on air transportation, water taxis and bicycle and boat rentals on the island.

A Route to Follow

A quadrangular route around Denman begins at the terminus of the ferry from Vancouver Island. It cuts directly across the island, skirts the western shore to the ferry terminal for Hornby Island, backtracks to McFarlane Road, which cuts through the wooded southern end of the island, and returns along the eastern shore to the starting point at the ferry terminal.

After climbing the hill from the ferry, the first thing a visitor to Denman might do is stop and savour "downtown" Denman, at the corner of Denman and North-west roads. Within a block of this corner is a grocery store and cafe, the Denman Island Museum, the elementary school, a church, an arts and crafts gallery, and the community centre. Other services, including bed and breakfast establishments, are located within a few blocks.

The Denman Island General Store is a focal point of the community, serving gas and groceries, along with lively conversation in the busy cafe. The false-fronted wooden building is of 1910 vintage. The post office was moved here in 1918 and still operates out of the store.

Across from the store, St. Saviour's Anglican Church is surrounded by lawns and trees. It was built in 1914 by local parishioners. The cornerstone is made of Denman Island sandstone milled from the quarry that operated here from 1908 to 1914. The quarry operated successfully for some years, and had its own railway leading to the waterfront where scows tied up at the company's private dock.

A short distance away on North-west Road, the community centre is a good example of how Denman Islanders incorporate the old and the new in a unique mix. The central part of the community centre dates back to the early years of this century. Over the years the building has undergone a series of modifications and restorations, and it now houses a library and a theatre that accommodates visiting and local talent. The entrance portico is supported with whimsical sculptures made from tree limbs by Denman Island sculptor Michael Dennis.

To take the main route around the island, continue along Denman Road, following signs to the Hornby Island ferry. The attractive old homes, farms and buildings on Denman contribute to the comfortable rural atmosphere and sense of continuity with the past that permeates Denman. They are located throughout the island, but many can be seen along the main route. Just past the intersection of Denman Road with North-west Road, there is a fine old shingled home which operated for many years as a bed and

Community centre, with wood sculptures.

81

breakfast. It was built around 1914 by one of the island's early loggers. Not far from here, at the junction with Lacon Road, is a large clapboard home built around 1908 for Sam Dumaresq, the owner of the sandstone quarry.

Denman Road climbs steeply for the next stretch, the only major impediment for cyclists on this route. From the crest it gradually flattens out, to where it becomes East Road on the eastern shore. Near the top of the hill is the United Church. Although it is the island's oldest church, built in 1889, renovations and additions have perhaps too successfully disguised its age.

For a few kilometres the road passes through a clearcut area — perhaps the only part of Denman that is not unusually attractive. The local cemetery is next: a quiet stroll through its well-tended grounds reveals a roster of names that are repeated on roads, bays, and lakes throughout the island — Millard, Mackenzie, Scott, Chalmers, Isbister, Swan, Patterson, McNaught, McFarlan, Fulton, Pickles, McGee, Lacon, Corrigal and more. The number of Scots who settled on Denman in the early days earned it the name Little Orkney for some years.

Shortly after passing a turnoff to the left for Fillongley Provincial Park, the main road reaches the eastern shore of the island and turns south, becoming — appropriately enough — East Road. (This same no-nonsense approach also produced roads named Denman and North-west.)

Near this corner there are several fine examples of early farm architecture.

The drive along the east shore is attractive, with views of Hornby Island to the east and pastoral farmlands and forested tracts to the west. Those

Rural flavour on Denman Island roads.

82

who want to dawdle and enjoy the scenery are advised to pull aside if they find themselves at the head of an ever-lengthening cortege of vehicles. This is the main route for commuters to the Hornby Island ferry at Gravelly Bay and traffic moves at a fair clip. Between ferries, and in the off-season, those who wish to travel at a sedate pace reclaim the roads.

Near McFarlane Road, settlement increases and there are several beach accesses that make pleasant stopping places. The one with the most convenient parking is a few metres before the junction of McFarlane Road and East Road. The beach is walkable for some distance each way, with good views of the terraced slopes of Mount Geoffrey on Hornby Island. Offshore islets of conglomerate sandstone are connected to the beach at low tide, forming tidal pools where gulls and crows stalk their prey.

The ferry to Hornby, at Gravelly Bay, marks the end of this portion of the main route. Gravelly it may be, but the bay is little more than a slight indentation in the coast. The shoreline of large sandstone conglomerate formations backed by mossy knolls can be explored while waiting for the ferry to arrive. There is a good concrete boat launch here.

To continue on the main route, backtrack from the ferry dock to McFarlane Road and turn left onto McFarlane, which cuts through the forested southern portion of the island. Although the land around McFarlane has been subdivided, few homes are visible along the 2.5-kilometre length of the road. Where McFarlane intersects with Lacon Road, turn right and complete the route on Lacon, following along the western shore.

Just past the turn, you may glimpse the black barrels of a longline oyster lease just offshore. This western coast of Denman is virtually lined with oyster leases, and many of the beach accesses reveal either the floats of the longline leases or signs stating that picking oysters at lease locations is illegal. Some oyster lease operators erect signs that tell you to keep off the beach, but that's not necessary as long as you stick close to the high tide line, in order not to damage the seed oysters.

At Millard Road a steep (13-percent grade), rough gravel road allows beach access. There is a rough boat launch here, but you'd need a rugged vehicle to manage the road, especially with a trailer in tow.

Lacon Road provides almost continuous views of Baynes Sound and the shoreline and mountains of Vancouver Island. Settlement increases as the road approaches the junction with Denman Road, where you turn left to return to the ferry dock and your starting point.

What the Main Route Misses

Fillongley Provincial Park

Fillongley is a 23-hectare park that combines beach, a marshy estuary, a fine forest with old-growth firs, and the remnants of what was once a large estate. Established in 1954, land for the park was donated to the province by George Beadnell, who died in 1958. Beadnell was one of the first dozen pioneers on Denman, a man who loved the land and the social life of the island. Local histories relate that the inscription over the huge fireplace in his home — made of beach rocks he collected himself — read "Hunc coeant flammae rustus fulgore sodales" (Hither let my friends foregather in my ruddy firelight glow).

Over the years Beadnell developed Fillongley into one of the most beautiful estates in the islands. A long winding driveway led from the house through the huge trees to the roadside, where the entrance was marked with lovely intricate gateways made of bent wood. The plants for extensive gardens of trees, shrubs and flowers were grown in a greenhouse near the house. He even built a tennis court, bowling green and a clubhouse.

After Beadnell's death the park remained undeveloped for some years, and the large house and other facilities fell into disrepair. Eventually the house was burnt to the ground by park authorities, the greenhouse was destroyed and the well filled in. Of the estate, only the broad sweep of meadow remains, with its magnificent spreading beechnut and other cultivated varieties of tree. The grounds are kept manicured by parks personnel and by phantom pruners, locals who nip in to tend to the trees and bushes when the need arises.

The park seems to exercise a benign influence over its regular users. One of Beadnell's conditions for the donation of Fillongley to the province was that he be buried on the property, and his grave is situated by a shady path in the park. Appreciators of his generosity often leave offerings of leaves, flowers or shell arrangements by the grave marker. Others observe

Fillongley Provincial Park.

another ritual, saying a quiet "Thank you George," as they pass the gravesite.

Where the earth is disturbed along the forest paths, you can see bits of broken shell mixed in with the earth, shell heaps left by native Indians over many years of use. To the right of the park is an oyster lease, but there are plenty of clams and oysters along the park foreshore, which also offers pleasant walking for several kilometres along the shore.

There are pit toilets, a pump for drinking water and ten campsites at the park. Camping arrangements are a little unusual, as the sites are lined up side by side at a paved parking area, but tents can be pitched nearby under the trees for a little more privacy.

To get to Fillongley, take Denman Road from the ferry and turn left at Swan Road, then right at Beadnell Road. The park is to your immediate left as you reach the water.

Boyle Point Provincial Park

This undeveloped park has no facilities, but it offers several kilometres of good trails through open coastal forest to cliffside points overlooking Eagle Rock and Chrome Island lighthouse. At very low tide the passage between Denman and Eagle Rock dries. Steep trails from Denman allow access to Eagle Rock, where petroglyphs are reportedly visible, although many more petroglyphs have been documented at Chrome Island. Boyle Point is one of the favourite fishing spots on Denman, so boats often congregate here.

From the cliff overlooking the lighthouse, eagles soar at eye level and turkey vultures are sometimes sighted. The views of Vancouver Island and the open waters to the south are breathtaking. Far below, the pristine buildings of the lighthouse cling to the island.

Chrome Island (formerly called Yellow Rock) is named for its steep buff-coloured sandstone cliffs, streaked with the guano of nesting cormorants. The first lighthouse was built here in 1891, but disaster struck in the early morning hours of December 16, 1900. Bound for the Orient, the *Alpha*, a 68-metre-long iron steamer, had left Victoria the previous afternoon with her cargo of coal and salmon. Heavily overloaded and skippered by Captain F.H. Yorke, who was inexperienced on the West Coast, the *Alpha* foundered on the rocks of Chrome Island in a blinding snowstorm just after midnight. As huge waves washed over the deck, Quartermaster Anderson plunged over the side with a rope and managed to scale the rocks and attach the line. At least two dozen of the crew members made it ashore using the lifeline; the captain and eight seamen spurned the rope and perished when the mast they were clinging to broke and was washed away.

Chickadee Lake

Chickadee is a small lake in the northern part of Denman. Although access is somewhat difficult, the lake is used by some locals for swimming. It is mud-bottomed and there are reeds and lily pads on much of the perimeter. There's a good supply of cutthroat trout, which reach 35 to 40 centimetres in length. Local groups do not actively encourage use of Chickadee Lake (or Graham Lake to the south) because they are reservoirs for island drinking water.

To get there, take North-west Road, off Denman Road, and turn right onto Lake Road. Within about one kilometre, just where the lake becomes visible to your left through the trees, an unmarked driveway and turnaround gives access to the lake.

Emergencies and Information

Denman Island is served by Courtenay RCMP. Emergency numbers are found at the front of the telephone directory, or the operator may be able to help.

Travel Infocentres at Parksville and Courtenay, the Denman Island General Store and other local businesses can provide information about the island.

Camping and Accommodation

The only provincial campground on the island is at Fillongley Provincial Park, which has just 10 sites. Many campers find themselves stranded when they arrive too late at the campground. A number of bed and

St. Saviour's Anglican Church.

breakfast establishments serve the island. For current accommodations, check with the local chamber of commerce, or look in Tourism B.C.'s annual *Accommodations* booklet, described in Chapter One.

Shopping and Services

The Denman Island General Store carries a modest selection of most amenities and sells gas and propane. A liquor outlet and post office are located in the store. Real estate services are nearby. As well as the craft gallery next to the community centre, Denman Island has a number of excellent artists and craftspeople who work from home studios. Watch for signs as you drive around the island.

Recreation and Events

Check with local businesses or the Travel Infocentre for details on rental of bicycles or other recreational equipment.

Annual events include Denman Days, a baseball tournament that is usually held each August. The Farmers' Market, a fall fair held in the community centre at the beginning of September, includes a dance, sale of crafts and judging of foods. The Christmas craft sale organized for November each year highlights local artisans and draws from surrounding areas.

Hiking — Seashore Walks, Forest Paths

Denman has few marked hiking trails, but its quiet roads and long gravel beaches offer a variety of environments for hiking. See also The Main Route, for information about beach accesses along the main island roads, as well as What the Main Route Misses, for information on hiking at Fillongley and Boyle Point provincial parks.

North-west Road Beach Access

There are two beach accesses off North-west Road that offer pleasant walking with views of Baynes Sound and Vancouver Island. The first is at Scott Road. There is an oyster lease here, so be thoughtful about keeping to the high tide line when walking where the oyster lease is located. To get to the second beach access, continue farther north along North-west Road to Gladstone Way Road. The road ends in a turnaround and parking area. Large signs warn of private property, but look for a marked public path beside the private property. You can hike along this beautiful sand and gravel shoreline at low tide, past the gravel beaches of Henry Bay (occupied by oyster leases) to Longbeak Point and, if the tide is very low, on to Sandy Island. See Paddling and Small Boating for a description of Sandy Island Provincial Marine Park.

Reginald Road Beach Access

This road leads to beaches at the southern, less inhabited end of Denman. To get there, turn right onto Reginald Road off McFarlane Road. Reginald is a gravel road just under 2 kilometres long that ends in a wide turnaround where you can park. The path to the beach is short and steep.

Rock formations at the south end of the island.

Rock formations on the beach are interesting: shale sandwiched between sandstone layers, and long, geometric, shiny black rocks that snake out into the water like dragons' backbones. Tubular grey concretions — harder material that does not erode as quickly as the surrounding rock — emerge from the sandstone; some have broken free and can be found among the beach pebbles. Although concretions usually form around organic matter, they are not often a good source of fossils.

There are no homes along the waterfront, which rises in steep bluffs to the south, and there is a strong sense of remoteness here. Often the only company is ospreys, eagles, herons and seabirds.

Lacon Road Beach Access

Follow Lacon Road just over 1.5 kilometres past the intersection with McFarlane Road, where Hilton Road (unmarked) veers sharply toward the beach and a parking area. There are oyster leases to the right and left. Just around the point to the south is a grassy estuary where a stream enters the sea. Metcalfe Bay, just over a kilometre north, has a sandy beach.

Paddling and Small Boating — Day Trips or Overnight

Sandy Island Provincial Marine Park

Distance: 10 nautical miles round trip. *Launching*: Boat launch near ferry dock.

The sandy beaches of this 32-hectare marine park are an excellent destination for day trips and overnight camping. Just off the northwest end of Denman, the islands are connected to each other and to Denman at extremely low tides, when a sandbar extends far to the north.

A variety and abundance of birds inhabit the park, including herons and eagles. Wildflowers grow on the islets in spring and the shores vary from mudflats to sand and pebble beaches. Campers often pitch their tents in the lee of the trees on Sandy Island, for protection from southeasterlies or northwesterlies.

In most weather, Sandy Island is an easy paddle in sheltered waters from the boat launch at the ferry dock.

Boyle Point

Distance: 3 nautical miles return. *Launching*: Boat launch at Gravelly Bay.

An afternoon of paddling and exploration can take you from the ferry dock at Gravelly Bay to Boyle Point. At Boyle Point, steep paths lead to trails through the park. Just west of the point, there is a sandy bay with large sandstone rock formations below the high-tide line.

Visitors are permitted to tour the Chrome Island lighthouse, but arrangements must be made beforehand; don't paddle up unannounced. Call the Canadian Coast Guard, which is listed in telephone directories. Because of the steep, clifflike shoreline of Chrome Island, it is difficult to go ashore from a boat, particularly at low tide.

When You Arrive by Private Boat

The shoreline of Denman Island is not hospitable to boaters. There are few nooks and crannies to offer shelter along its coast, it has no safe, all-weather anchorages, and the government wharf by the ferry dock has fallen into disrepair.

Residents anchor in several places along the west coast, which has reasonable summer anchorage. There is good temporary anchorage at Sandy Island Provincial Marine Park, in the lee of Sandy Island, although it is not protected from southeast winds. Henry Bay, to the south, is exposed to the west and northwest, but there is good protection from the south.

If the wind rises, there are good anchorages nearby, at Deep Bay on Vancouver Island and Ford Cove on Hornby Island.

Denman Fishing

The area around Denman and Hornby islands is considered by some to be one of the finest fishing areas in the Gulf Islands. Tidal streams in the channels are relatively slow, and anglers can usually find a protected spot to fish.

Komass Bluffs

Launching: Gravelly Bay.

These 60- to 90-metre sand cliffs are often fished by those trying to avoid the more crowded conditions of Comox Bar or Norris Rocks. Chinook and coho fishing is good here through summer and fall. Fish in 35 to 60 metres of water.

Try driftfishing or trolling for chinooks early in the year, with May and June the hot times for summer-run Puntledge River chinooks. Coho fishing can be excellent from August right through to early November.

Chrome Island

Launching: Gravelly Bay.

Those wishing a shorter run to fishing territory might try the dropoff around Chrome Island. From June to September, coho gather here; the big northern coho arrive in September.

Sandy Island Marine Park

Launching: near the ferry terminal.

Much of Lambert Channel affords good fishing. Near the northwest tip of Denman, fish around Palliser Rock, at depths of 20 metres or more. Driftfishing or trolling are the preferred methods.

Denman Scuba Diving

Chrome Island Lighthouse

Boat dive. Launching: Gravelly Bay boat launch.

The wreck of the *Alpha*, a 68-metre steamer that went down off Chrome Island during a December gale in 1900, still attracts divers to where it rests in 10 to 12 metres of water. It has been so spread by storms and pilfered by divers that little remains, but the hulk is still visible. The

The Chrome Island lighthouse.

91

anchor was recovered in 1972 and installed near the ferry terminal as a memorial.

This is a sheltered dive with only light tidal currents if divers stay in the shallows on the east side of the lighthouse. The shoreline here provides a number of small interesting dives. On sandy flats at a depth of 10 to 12 metres, there are sandstone caves where wolf-eels and octopi lurk and sea pens can be seen. Tube-dwelling anemones and giant nudibranchs thrive here, away from the rapid currents of the channels. Moon snails can be seen in the sandy areas and large sunflowerstars, over half a metre in diameter, are common.

Hornby Island

Sculpted Sandstone Shores

 For years, Hornby Island was a well-kept secret. Travellers, mindful of the logistics of taking a ferry from Vancouver Island to Denman, then another from Denman to Hornby, often bypassed Hornby for other more accessible destinations. The low-key rural atmosphere, the riding and hiking trails of Mount Geoffrey, the white sand beaches and aquamarine waters of Tribune Bay, and the voluptuous sandstone formations and fossil-strewn beaches surrounding the island were enjoyed by an initiated few.

Today the barriers have been breached. Hornby, 30 square kilometres in size, has a permanent population of more than 800 — a number that

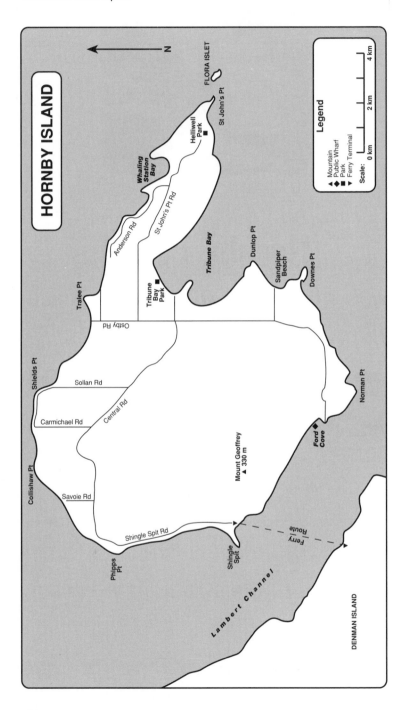

HORNBY ISLAND

FLORA ISLET

St John's Pt

Helliwell
Park

Whaling
Station
Bay

Anderson Rd

St John's Pt Rd

Tribune Bay

Dunlop Pt

Sandpiper
Beach

Downes Pt

Tralee Pt

Tribune
Bay
Park

Ostby Rd

Shields Pt

Sollan Rd

Central Rd

Carmichael Rd

Collishaw Pt

Norman Pt

Ford
Cove

Mount Geoffrey
▲ 330 m

Savoie Rd

Shingle Spit Rd

Phipps
Pt

Shingle
Spit

Ferry Route

Lambert Channel

DENMAN ISLAND

Legend

▲ Mountain
◆ Public Wharf
■ Park
▶ Ferry Terminal

Scale:

0 km   2 km   4 km

doubles or even triples in summer. But these summer visitors strain the facilities of the island: accommodation is scarce, fresh water is at a premium, and the social structure changes. Some enjoy the heightened summer activity, and even at its peak, there are secluded trails and beaches. But visitors who seek the underlying nature of Hornby Island are well advised to travel here when the tourists have gone.

Being the outer of the two islands, Hornby was not settled as quickly as Denman. At a time when most settlers got around by rowboat or dugout canoe, the crossing of Lambert Channel, between Denman and Hornby, was a considerable barrier. Perhaps that early isolation and the legacy of the first pioneers bred the initiative and independence that is evident on the island today.

The Co-op Store and Hornby's recycling system are two examples of how islanders have cooperated to overcome common difficulties. Long before the concept of recycling garbage entered the popular domain, in the early 1970s, Hornby Islanders devised their own system to eliminate their garbage. Everyone on Hornby — from day visitors and campers to permanent residents — participates in the recycling program. It is so well organized that once they have accustomed themselves to the system, visitors often go away wondering why it hasn't always been done this way in their own communities.

The Co-op Store has become one of the central meeting places of the island. It is owned by its members but is open to everyone. From its early days, when it was a small outlet established to serve the immediate needs

Welded sculptures like these can be seen in several places around Hornby.

of residents, the store has blossomed, selling a wide variety of goods to accommodate all customers.

There are many artists on Hornby, but the island is known especially for its potters, who number among B.C.'s top artisans. It is not hard to imagine, when exploring the beaches around Hornby, that they are inspired by the magical creations of nature that surround them.

The most imposing natural feature of Hornby is Mount Geoffrey, which rises abruptly in the west to over 300 metres. A rich agricultural plateau that spreads along the foot of the mountain encompasses most of the western edge of the island. Much of this plain, with the exception of residential subdivisions near Shields Point and Sandpiper Beach, is protected within B.C.'s agricultural land reserve.

On the southeast side of the island, Tribune Bay is hammered by huge winter waves, pushed by winds that blow across nearly 145 kilometres of open water. The particles carried by the waves, the pounding on the sandstone shelf, and the deep shape of the bay have contributed to the formation of Tribune's fine sand beach, which rivals many on the southwest coast.

Getting There

The ferry to Hornby Island makes the 15-minute crossing between Gravelly Bay on Denman Island and Shingle Spit on Hornby Island several times a day but shuts down around dinner time. It can be crowded on summer weekends and other holiday times, so don't get caught out. B.C. Ferries, local businesses or the Travel Infocentre can provide ferry schedules.

Check in the telephone directory (Hornby produces its own directory) or with local businesses for information regarding taxis, and bicycle, boat and sailboard rentals on the island.

A Route to Follow

Hornby Island no longer has a road that encircles the island, but its main artery cuts from the ferry terminal at Shingle Spit across to the heart of the island, the Co-op Store. From there, it turns south and continues to Ford Cove, and another arm branches north to Helliwell Provincial Park and communities near Whaling Station Bay.

There are a lot of cyclists, hikers and horseback riders on Hornby, so pay particular attention on the island's narrow winding roads. Local architecture — both old and new — also demands attention. This is an island of fine wooden homes built by early settlers, of old weatherbeaten barns, of sod-roofed cabins and original modern designs that often incorporate rock detailing and sod roofs.

Immediately upon disembarking from the ferry, there is a small resort area with a cluster of services overlooking Shingle Spit. From here Central Road follows the shoreline, with views of Denman Island and Vancouver Island. On the other side, the 330-metre face of Mount Geoffrey seems to drop in a straight line to the pastoral flatlands below.

The Heatherbell barn is about 2 kilometres from the ferry dock. This tall, vertically planked barn is almost a hundred years old; local historians report that people came from both Denman and Hornby islands for the barn-raising, making the huge beams by hand. The barn was used for dairy cattle operations until 1977, when it was bought by a Hornby Island sculptor. Farther along, just before the road turns inland, there is another historic barn, now returning to the soil, and a well-preserved house, built around the same time.

At Sollans Road there is a cluster of service structures, including a daycare centre, RCMP, health centre, and — the most impressive — a community centre. This building is worth a stop to see at close hand. The fine wood and stone detailing, the incorporation of driftwood pieces and the sod roof combine to create a building that is both visually arresting and representative of the community.

The junction by the Co-op Store is about 9 kilometres from the ferry terminal. A meeting place for locals and visitors, the main component of the complex is the Co-op Store, with its broad verandah, where people stop to pass the time of day and check out the notice board. Inside, there is a wide and completely eclectic selection of grocery and dry goods. Hornby Islanders are rightfully proud of the store, which allows members a great degree of independence and control over island supplies.

Weathered barns are seen everywhere on the island.

97

Outside the store, a harmonious hodgepodge of craft outlets and eateries is aesthetically bound by shingle and wood log construction, and physically connected by wooden walkways. The walkways and outdoor seating are always crowded with a mixture of islanders and visitors, from toddlers to seniors. Horses are often tied up near the road and dogs wait patiently nearby, as the enticing fresh-food fragrance wafts in the air. Jewelry, pottery and clothing displayed in the tiny stores tempt shoppers.

It is a short, half-kilometre jaunt down Salt Spray Road to the Tribune Bay beach access (Tribune Bay is described later in this section), but to continue along the main route, you have a choice: follow Central Road as it takes a right turn at the co-op store and go to Ford Cove, or turn left onto St. John Point Road, eventually ending at Helliwell Provincial Park. In either case, you will be retracing your route to return to your starting point.

Past the Co-op Store, Central Road passes through an area of broad fields and weathered barns. Open fields to the left run down to Little Tribune Bay with the bluffs of Helliwell in the distance. Eventually the road climbs to dry uplands where arbutus cling to rocky ledges. Huge maples and Garry oaks frame beautiful views of the farmlands below, and beyond Denman Island to the snow-crowned mountains of Vancouver Island. From here the road descends steeply, passing the well-appointed buildings of the farm seen from the road above.

Ford Cove is a sleepy little corner that catches the sun from early in the morning until sunset. The land here was preempted by one of Hornby's first two settlers, George Ford. Henry Maud settled at Tribune Bay, and according to local history books, the two friends planned to eventually acquire the entire island between them. Their plans were interrupted when other settlers arrived on Hornby, but Ford managed to acquire over 500 hectares south of the cove named for him.

This is the only all-weather port on Hornby Island. A store, campsites,

The Hornby Island Community Centre.

cottages and fresh water are available here. There is a steep, rough gravel boat launch by the government dock.

The shoreline near Ford Cove is a place to stop and explore. Large sandstone slabs south of the docks are great for sunbathing and you can walk about a kilometre along a shore with beautiful sandstone formations to Norman Point.

To continue, retrace your route to the Co-op Store and continue straight,

Hoodoo at Tribune Bay.

99

along St. John Point Road, which forms the boundary for Tribune Bay Provincial Park. The park comprises 95 hectares of beach, open meadows and forested flatlands. There are two entrances to the park from the road. The first, about half a kilometre from the store, has a parking lot, changing rooms, pit toilets, drinking water and a few picnic tables above the beach. The second entrance, perhaps a kilometre farther along St. John Point Road, is for pedestrians only and is closer to the site of an old lodge. There are tennis courts and a covered barbecue area here. Trails connect the two main sections of the park.

The land around Tribune Bay was first preempted by Henry Maud in the 1880s. In 1928, part of his estate was bought by a Vancouver businessman who built a resort lodge overlooking Tribune Bay, using the old Maude farmhouse as a kitchen. Early brochures describe the facilities in glowing terms. Holidaymakers were assured that they would "delight in bathing in WARM, GLEAMING WATERS" and would "have ABSOLUTE FREEDOM FROM MOSQUITOES." Under the American Plan rates, two adults could have a cabin and all their meals for $17.50 per week. The lodge was operated successfully for many years by a succession of owners until the province, with the help of the Devonian Foundation, acquired it for a park in 1978. The original lodge is used for group activities.

The white sand and clear aquamarine waters of this bay are unique in the northern Gulf Islands. With its long gentle slope and sun-warmed water, it's a great place to take children. At low tide the rocky foreshore provides hours of pleasurable exploration of tide pools.

The unusual rock formations at Spray Point, the rocky peninsula jutting into the bay, are sandstone with a granite cap. Wind and wave erosion have formed them into hoodoos and other magical shapes. It's easy to imagine these shores as the archaeological ruins of some ancient culture.

Past the second entrance to the park, the next point of interest is Whaling Station Bay. There are a couple of beach accesses with easy parking just off St. John Point Road.

The shoreline above Whaling Station Bay is now all privately owned but, as its name implies, it was once the scene of a whale processing plant, in the days when large whales were a common sight in the waters of Georgia Strait. Whaling, which began on the Pacific coast in about 1840, was originally based near San Francisco. In the late 1860s several small operations were started in B.C. waters. Dawson Whaling Company set up the first station at Whaletown, on Cortes Island, in 1869. It operated there for just one year, then moved to Hornby Island under the name B.C. Whaling Company. By 1872, the big whales were gone, decimated by the whaling ships, and the company was bankrupt. All the company's holdings, including 40 hectares preempted at Whaling Station Bay, with a wharf and several sheds, was auctioned off. All evidence of this operation has disappeared, but remnants of the whaling industry — giant vertebrae and other whalebones — have washed up here over the years.

Whaling Station Bay has a fine sandy beach backed by flat sandstone slabs that soak up the sun and are great places for loafing. The beach, which looks toward Texada Island, is used mainly by locals and is less crowded than the popular Tribune Bay. Waterfowl bob in the water just offshore and the sleek, round heads of harbour seals can be seen occasionally. There is a variety of interesting old and new architecture around the beach, and the huge conglomerate rocks at Cape Gurney make a good destination for a walk. It is a wonderful place to spend a day or an hour.

Just past the bay, a right turn onto Helliwell Road leads to Helliwell Provincial Park, established in 1966 as a result of a donation of land by John Helliwell. Facilities at the 69-hectare park include pit toilets, an information shelter, a parking lot and a trail system.

From here you can retrace the route to the junction with Central Road at the Co-op Store, and return on Central Road to your starting point at the ferry.

What the Main Route Misses

The magnificent beaches of Hornby Island are invitations to explore. Even in midsummer, it is possible to find solitude at some of the beaches, where you can look for fossils, observe wildlife or simply breathe in the fresh salt air and hear the soothing rhythm of the waves. There are numerous beach accesses around Hornby; they are usually denoted by a wide lane to the water and a red and white sign that prohibits overnight camping.

The following beach accesses are in the order they would fall if you were taking the main route around the island.

Phipps Point

Phipps Point is the site of an old government landing built for a passenger service to Comox, in the days when transportation links were still being forged between Hornby and the other islands. The cement jetty juts out into the water, and a runway beside the pier makes a good boat launch at high tide; light boats can be launched at a lower tide.

The beach to the west of here is occupied by an oyster lease, but there is good shellfish harvesting to the east, among the rocky outcroppings all the way to Collishaw Point. Fossils are also found along this stretch of beach. The best places to find fossils are in well-exposed shale beaches, which are plentiful on Hornby.

You can get to Phipps Point from Shingle Spit Road. Turn west onto Central Road (about 2.5 kilometres from the ferry terminal), a short, steep road with a parking space and turnaround at the bottom.

Collishaw Point

At Collishaw Point a shallow ledge extends out from the shore for almost 1.5 kilometres, much of it revealed at low tide. You can walk far out onto the flats, maneuvering around boulders. The larger boulders are hazardous to boaters when high water covers them.

There are plenty of oysters and clams for the picking at Collishaw Point — some say they are the best on Hornby — and the area is especially noted for its fossils. Eagles and herons feed here at low tide, and it's possible to walk to within a few metres of large rocks where dozens of seals regularly bask.

To get to Collishaw Point, turn onto Savoie Road from Central Road. Less than half a kilometre long, the road ends in a grassy turnaround. The overgrown path to the beach follows alongside a fenced farm where many "no trespassing" signs are posted. It's about a five-minute walk to the beach; Collishaw Point is to the right as you reach the water.

Shields Point (Grassy Point)

Follow Carmichael Road to its end and turn right onto Harwood. Within a short distance there is a large parking area that opens out into a grassy field. Below the headland is a pebble beach. There is a good boat launch here, accessible at all but low tides. Residents' boats line the driveway. Texada and Lasqueti islands lie to the east; Quadra and Cortes islands can be seen to the north.

From Shields Point, you can walk south to Galleon Beach. This is a lovely secluded beach with few homes, large sandstone formations and tide pools.

From Grassy Point, you can return along the same route, via Harwood and Carmichael, or continue along Harwood to Sollan Road, which connects to Central Road.

Tralee Point and Fowler Road Beach Access

To get to this beach access, go almost to the end of Ostby Road and turn right onto Fowler Road. Continue to a parking area at the end of the road. A path leads through the forest to a fairly steep trail to the beach. There are offshoots of the trail here but they may lead to private property, so be careful not to trespass. Nearby there is a heronry: the acidic smell of guano permeates the white-splashed forest and alerts hikers to the huge nests high in the trees.

From the beach, it is possible to walk to the north around Tralee Point, with its large round boulders, sandstone ledges and conglomerate outcroppings. Past the point, several petroglyphs are faintly visible on a sandstone ledge near the high tide line.

Anderson Road

This road, which parallels the coast for a couple of kilometres between Whaling Station Bay and Sea Dollar Road, runs through an area of homes with an interesting variety of architectural detailing. There are many beach accesses along the way; watch for the red and white signs prohibiting overnight camping, which indicate a beach access. Anderson Road is a dead end, so you'll have to backtrack to St. John Point Road.

Sandpiper Beach

Sandpiper Beach, between Dunlop and Downes points, is a narrow sandy beach lined with driftwood. Always beautiful, it is most interesting at low tide, when long fingers of shale are revealed, extending in parallel lines out to sea, like miniature breakwaters. From here you can see the whitened cliffs of Helliwell to the east. The area around Sandpiper Beach is unusual for Hornby, as it is a densely developed subdivision of suburban homes, but it doesn't intrude on the beauty of the beach, which is often deserted.

To get to the beach, take Sandpiper Drive off Central Road. Where it meets Porpoise Crescent, there is a large grassy area with a parking area just to the left.

Emergencies and Information

The island has a seasonal RCMP detachment and is otherwise policed by Courtenay RCMP. There is a medical clinic on the island. Emergency numbers are at the front of the telephone directory, or the operator can likely provide assistance.

Businesses on the island can usually provide information about events and facilities. The Co-op Store sells maps and books and has a bulletin board where community information is posted, and personal messages can be passed on.

Camping and Accommodation

There is no provincial campground on Hornby, but there are several private campgrounds. Reservations are well advised, as Hornby is a popular summer destination. For current listings of private campgrounds, bed and breakfast outlets, resorts and inns, check local directories or Tourism B.C.'s *Accommodations* booklet, described in Chapter One.

Shopping and Services

The main shopping area on Hornby is the Co-op Store and Crafts Market. The store is completely stocked with everything from fresh pasta and organic juice to colas, newspapers and deli products. (It also has a good supply of bottled water, as there can be severe water shortages on the island in summer, and the available water might be sulfurous.) The hardware department caters to campers and islanders. The post office is located in the store, and there is a gas station at the complex. There is no liquor store on Hornby Island, but there's a pub beside the ferry terminal.

At the outdoor Crafts Market, a variety of prepared food is available along with a good sampling of island artistry. Other commercial outlets, including grocery store, restaurants, galleries and boutiques, a pub, and shower and laundromat facilities, are located at Ford Cove and near the ferry landing at Shingle Spit. Fresh produce is sold from local greenhouses.

Many of Hornby's potters, jewellers and other artists welcome visitors to their studios; a day can easily be consumed visiting studios around the island.

Recreation and Events

Hornby's annual midsummer Festival of the Arts, with music, theatre, comedy, film and dance, attracts performers from across Canada. Every second year, on even years, the Hornby Fair features arts and crafts, music and performances on an outdoor stage at the island's school grounds. Check with locals for other events.

Softball tournaments are regularly scheduled in the summer at Joe King Park, with leagues from Vancouver Island and neighbouring islands competing. Community dances are held on major occasions throughout the year at the Community Hall, and there has been a polar bear swim at Shingle Spit for more than a decade.

Look in the telephone directory or check with local outlets for information on fishing charters, scuba diving, nature and sightseeing tours, kayak tours and horseback riding on Hornby.

Hiking — Cliffside Trails, Fossil Beaches

Some of Hornby's best walking is along the beaches, and the beach accesses are detailed in What the Main Route Misses. Established hiking trails in Helliwell Provincial Park and along the benches of Mount Geoffrey are described below. Locals may also be able to provide information on old logging roads and a network of trails in the regional park on the slopes of Mount Geoffrey.

Helliwell Provincial Park

A 5-kilometre, easy walking, circle trail leads along the Helliwell Bluffs and through some magnificent forest with huge Douglas firs. The bluffs are a mass of colour when carpeted with wildflowers in the spring. In summer, the dry, buff-coloured grasses ripple in the wind and form a stark contrast with the brilliant blue of the sky. From the trail along the cliff's edge, there are sweeping views of the open reaches of Georgia Strait and the mountains of the mainland and Vancouver Island to east and west. High above the sea, it's a particularly invigorating place to hike in a winter gale.

Pelagic cormorants nest on the cliffs below the bluffs. Occasionally, the acrid smell of the colonies below wafts up, but it is difficult to see the actual nesting sites from the bluff. In a few places it is possible to scramble down to the rocky shores for a swim. The many small rocky islets near Flora Islet are often covered with seals.

The trail begins and ends at the parking lot, where there are pit toilets and an information shelter. See The Main Route for more information about Helliwell Park.

Hiking the Helliwell Bluffs.

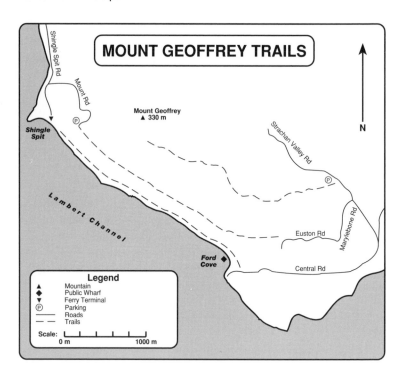

Mount Geoffrey

The distinctive shape of this land formation dominates the western aspect of Hornby Island. There are two well-defined trails along the western flank of the mountain, which rises to a height of 330 metres before dropping precipitously to an agricultural plateau that lies between the mountain and Shingle Spit Road. The trails along the benches of Mount Geoffrey have been created from the remains of old logging roads and are used by hikers, cyclists and horseback riders. A third trail to the summit is not well-marked and may require local help to find.

The Low Road

The lowest and easiest trail runs for over 3 kilometres between the Shingle Spit ferry terminal and Ford Cove. From Shingle Spit the trail begins with a short, steep incline in the bush just above the ferry terminal. The trailhead at the Ford Cove end is not marked either: watch for a narrow path to your left as you ascend the hill just outside Ford Cove. The entrance is overhung with blackberry bushes — in August you can fill up with juicy, sweet fruit before beginning your hike. The path runs alongside a fenced property for a short distance and then broadens out, with views of the water. Here the trail splits, leading to the water on the left — the only water access for the length of the trail. If you have difficulty finding the entrance, locals can help.

This is an easy walk through arbutus, firs, mossy boulders and a lush coastal understory of salal, huckleberry and Oregon grape. Huge outcroppings of conglomerate rock tower above the trail in places. There are enticing views from the low cliff to the water and foreshore below, but there is no easy way to get to the beach. It is about a 40-minute walk, one way, and you can either return the same way, or hike up to the beginning of the lower bench trail and complete the loop. Thirsty hikers will find refreshments at both ends of the lower trail.

The High Road

The bench trail is about a 50-minute walk between the end of Mount Road, near the ferry terminal, and Euston Road, above Ford Cove. It's easiest to find the start of this trail at the Ford Cove end. Take Strachan Road from Central Road, turn left on Marylebone, then right on Euston. The trail begins at the end of Euston. There are a number of private lots near the head of the trail and it is difficult in places to distinguish the public road from private driveways. It is particularly confusing if you approach from the north end of the trail. Be careful not to trespass.

At this south end of the trail, there are views over Ford Cove, of farmlands far below with ant-sized cattle, southern Denman Island, and the Chrome Island lighthouse. Toward Shingle Spit are great views of the ferry terminal and Shingle Spit, and Denman Island with Vancouver Island mountain peaks in the distance.

A hiker rests along the lowest trail on Mount Geoffrey.

The trail is forested, with huge, moss-draped maples and an occasional Douglas fir giant that escaped the loggers' saws. Alder has filled in some spots and there are some swampy areas with marsh grasses. Deer are a common sight. The path is wide and well packed, with no sheer or precipitous spots except at the lookouts. It's a favourite with horseback riders. Glimpses of the craggy face of the mountain above might tempt the more ambitious hikers to try the summit trail.

To begin at the Shingle Spit end, go about half a kilometre from the ferry terminal to Mount Road. Take Mount Road to a parking area at the end, where two paths enter the forest. The one closest to the water leads to bluffs overlooking the sea. The one farthest back from the ocean is the main trail, with several offshoots to mossy cliffside viewpoints.

To hike down to Ford Cove from the end of the trailhead at Euston Road takes about three-quarters of an hour. Just before Ford Cove, you can step onto the lower trail and follow the waterfront back to Shingle Spit.

The Summit Trail

The uppermost trail is for ambitious hikers, who are rewarded with spectacular views from dizzying heights over Denman Island and Baynes Sound to Vancouver Island. To reach the trailhead above Ford Cove, turn off Central Road onto Strachan Road. Less than a kilometre up Strachan

The south tip of Denman Island, seen from the higher trail on Mount Geoffrey.

Road, take a trail to the left and park by a gravel pit, where there is an unmarked trailhead. There is a network of trails here, but all are not marked and hikers may need help from locals in sorting them out. It's worth the effort.

Paddling and Small Boating — Islets, Reefs and Wildlife

The waters around Hornby are ideal for paddlers, with one very important proviso: there are few shelters on these shores and a watchful eye must be kept on the weather. With a 145-kilometre stretch of open water to the southeast, winds can rise quickly, and even a relatively slight wind can produce a nasty chop if it opposes the tidal flow. Early morning and evening generally provide calm periods in the day, with afternoon breezes.

Whaling Station Bay to Helliwell Bluffs

Distance: 4 nautical miles return. *Launching*: Whaling Station Bay.

The trip around Cape Gurney to St. John Point takes in some interesting small bays and reefs where there's a chance to see a variety of water birds, including cormorants, oldsquaw and black oystercatchers. The reefs around Flora Islet are home territory for one of four major groups of seals around the island. They haul out on the rocks and you can get quite close in a boat. In spring and winter, they share the rocks with sea lions, which often appear in the waters south of Hornby and Denman. Flora Islet is one of the places along the coast where six-gill sharks can be sighted, but they usually stay at a depth of at least 15 metres. (See the scuba-diving section.)

West of St. John Point, the Helliwell bluffs rise dramatically in sheer 60-metre-high cliffs of sandstone and conglomerate rock. A small boat is the best way to get a look at the nesting sites of about a hundred pairs of pelagic cormorants. Pigeon guillemots also nest here. Having got this far, you may want to continue another 1.5 nautical miles to cool off with a dip at the sandy beaches of Tribune Bay.

The shoreline along here is fully exposed to winds coming from Georgia Strait, so if a wind starts to blow, head to shore immediately.

Ford Cove to Shingle Spit

Distance: 3 nautical miles return. *Launching*: Ford Cove.

On a calm, sunny day, this is a leisurely paddle in the generally calm waters between Hornby and Denman. If you're hugging the shore you might see hikers on the trails of Mount Geoffrey, just above the shore. Lucky paddlers may see killer whales, which migrate through Lambert Channel on occasion. At Shingle Spit, refreshments are available before the paddle back. If a southeast wind springs up, it's best to head back to Ford Cove immediately, as it can be a stiff paddle to return against the wind.

Ford Cove to Norris Rocks

Distance: 2 nautical miles return. *Launching*: Ford Cove.

Past Norman Point, there are pastoral views of Hornby Island. Toby Islet and Norris Rocks are popular haulouts for seals. Gulls, cormorants and pigeon guillemots can also be seen here. Nearly 300 pairs of glaucous-winged seagulls nest at Norris Rocks during July and August. This is one of the most popular fishing spots around Hornby, so you might want to trail a line as you paddle along.

When You Arrive by Private Boat

Hornby is not visited much by yachtsmen because the anchorages are extremely limited. The coastline has almost no bays (with the obvious exception of Tribune), and though it is sometimes possible to anchor in the lee of Cape Gurney, Tralee Point and Shingle Spit, they offer only temporary anchorage if the wind is favourable.

Picturesque farm near Ford Cove.

Tribune Bay

There are usually a few boats in Tribune Bay in the summer. It is a generally safe anchorage, except during southeasterlies. The obvious charms of the bay outweigh the occasional need to head suddenly for more protected waters. Warm turquoise water laps over a fine sand beach that extends for over a kilometre from shore at low tide. There are interesting rock formations at Spray Point and trails, tennis courts and outbuildings at Tribune Bay Provincial Park. The Co-op Store, less than half a kilometre up Sea Spray Road, has all amenities.

Ford Cove

The breakwater and public wharf at Ford Cove makes it the only all-weather anchorage on the island. The store has gas and groceries, and various other services are located in the area. A trail leads to Shingle Spit, where there is a restaurant and pub. A beachfront walk in the other direction will take you to Norman Point.

Hornby Fishing

Shingle Spit

Launching: Boat launch at Shingle Spit.

Shingle Spit has been one of the favoured fishing areas on Hornby since the first settlement here, and it provides convenient, usually protected fishing, particularly in late June. Anglers fish both sides of the spit, or spincast from the end of the spit.

Collishaw Point

Launching: Shields Point.

Big salmon runs pass right by this point, and they move in to feed on the herring which come over the reef from June to August. Anglers troll or driftfish over the reef, staying in about 7 to 9 metres of water because of the shallows, which are dotted with large boulders. Later in the year, when the herring are larger, they move out to around the dropoff, and mooching becomes one of the most popular methods. Some anglers rake their own herring here.

Flora Islet

Launching: Whaling Station Bay or Shields Point.

Any calm summer evening brings out a raft of boats around Flora Islet. Like Shields Point, it is on the migration route for most of the salmon passing up and down Georgia Strait. Salmon are found on both the inside and outside of the main island. There is a well-known chinook hole on the inside of the main island, where anglers anchor in about 30 metres of water. Jigging for rockfish and ling cod can be productive at the dropoff. Trollers run in an arc from Whaling Station Bay south to the bottom of the reef around Flora Islet, up to the chinook hole and back to Whaling Station Bay. In August, Whaling Station Bay is popular for driftfishing and mooching along the kelp beds.

The open east side of Hornby is exposed to southeast winds, so be prepared to run for shore at short notice. Also keep an eye out for the flagged boats of divers around Flora Islet, particularly in late spring and summer.

Norris Rocks

Launching: Ford Cove.

The most popular fishing area on Hornby, Norris Rocks also attracts anglers from Vancouver Island and Denman. The reef is at the entrance to Lambert Channel and marks a shelf that continues to St. John Point. Driftfishing at the drop-off and over the shelf in about 12 to 18 metres of water is productive. The area is protected from all but southeasters.

If it is too windy to fish the outer reefs, the passage between Norris Rocks and Norman Point, and north to the ferry dock at Shingle Spit can be productive for salmon, rockfish and ling cod.

Ford Cove

Launching: Ford Cove.

There is a small reef off the mouth of Ford Cove that produces good-sized coho and chinook — to 12 kilograms through most of the year. The reef is a good spot for those staying at the cove, who might want to nip out for a short while, or if there is a southeast wind blowing.

Hornby Scuba Diving

There are several good dives around Hornby Island, but the island is best known for the six-gill sharks that bask in the summer months around Flora Islet. Check with local outlets for availability of air on the island.

Flora Islet

Boat dive. Launching: Ford Cove or Whaling Station Bay.

This area attracts divers from all over the world who come to swim with the 6-metre-long six-gill sharks. The sharks are normally found deep in the ocean, but from June to September they move slowly along an underwater ledge at the south end of Flora Islet. Some hypothesize that the sharks are somnolent with the unaccustomed warmth and that is why divers can swim among them and even touch them. Some divers say, though, that their tails are very sensitive and should be avoided. The sharks cruise slowly along the ledge, at a depth of 20 to 27 metres, and divers cruise along the wall in hopes of finding sharks.

If a shark doesn't appear, it's still an interesting dive. About 5 metres in from the edge of the dropoff, there are caves with wolf-eels, large skate and octopi. Herring school around the rocks and there are red snapper. At a depth of 18 to 20 metres there are low-lying kelp beds, small crimson anemones and some white plumose anemones.

Snapper Reef

Boat Dive. Launching: Ford Cove.

Snapper Reef is located in Lambert Channel near Ford Cove and has a channel marker above it. It is composed of long sandstone formations with overhangs, ledges and crevices. Lots of small marine life is visible here, at depths of 9 to 20 metres, including crimson anemones, grunt

Diver with six-gill shark near Flora Islet.

113

sculpins and tunicates. At about 24 metres it flattens out to a sand and mud bottom.

The reef was named for a gigantic red snapper that lived near the reef and had no fear of divers. One day a trigger-happy diver with a spear gun killed it, depriving all future divers of a chance to meet a snapper that was very probably in excess of 30 years old.

Divers should be experienced and should dive at slack tide, as the tidal streams run at 2 to 4 knots here.

Heron Rocks

Boat dive. Launching: Ford Cove.

Divers with varying levels of skill can dive at this point, where an amazing variety of underwater life can be seen from depths of 6 to 21 metres. Heron Rocks is a privately owned camping cooperative at Norman Point, so unless you have permission to cross private land, you must get to this shore dive with a boat.

From the base of the wall, at about 21 metres, you can work your way up along ledges where there are wolf eels and other fish. Marine life includes nudibranchs, corals, anemones, rock scallops and chitons.

Norman Point and Norris Rocks

Boat dive. Launching: Ford Cove.

Dozens of ling cod hang around these rocks. Kelp greenlings and rock cod keep them company, as well as plumose anemones, corals, rock scallops and starfish.

The current can be swift at the entrance to Lambert Channel; dive at slack tide only. The most abundant life is found near Norman Point in the high current areas. Out from Norman Point the channel is smooth and flat with small crevices and no large boulders. Divers find plenty of marine life in the small cracks.

Quadra Island

Tidal Streams and Inland Lakes

 Quadra Island lies at the entrance to the complex system of waterways and islands north of Georgia Strait. It is the second largest of all the inside islands, at 276 square kilometres, and has a population of some 2,200. Probably the most diverse of the northern Gulf Islands, it has a fairly rugged topography, which offers plenty of opportunities for outdoor exploration. Good trail systems provide access to wilderness areas in the largely uninhabited north end of the island. From mountains that rise to over 300 metres there are exciting views of Vancouver Island, the Discovery Islands and the mainland. Its inland waterway, the Main Lake Chain, is the largest freshwater system in the Gulf Islands.

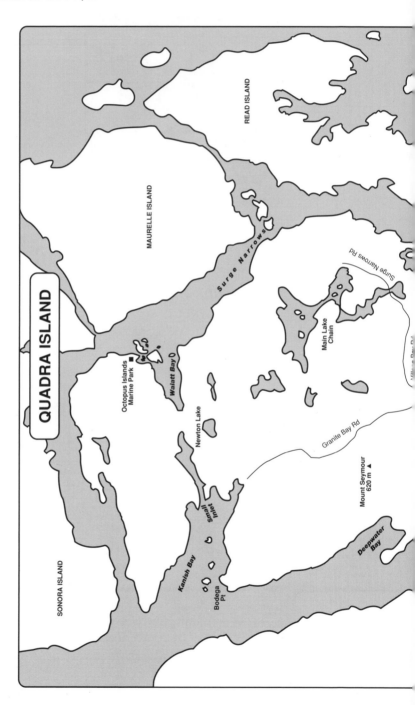

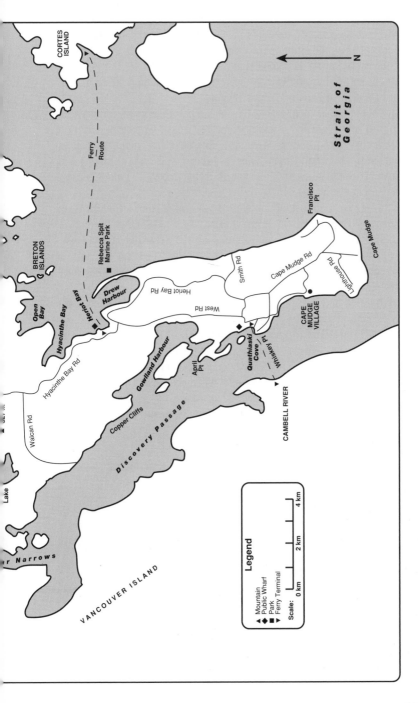

N

Strait of Georgia

CORTES ISLAND

Ferry Route

BRETON ISLANDS

Open Bay

Hyacinthe Bay

Rebecca Spit Marine Park

Francisco Pt

Heriot Bay

Drew Harbour

Smith Rd

Cape Mudge Rd

Cape Mudge

Heriot Bay Rd

Lighthouse Rd

West Rd

Hyacinthe Bay Rd

Walcan Rd

Gowlland Harbour

April Pt

Quathiaski Cove

Whiskey Pt

CAPE MUDGE VILLAGE

Copper Cliffs

Discovery Passage

CAMBELL RIVER

Lake

r Narrows

VANCOUVER ISLAND

Legend

Mountain
Public Wharf
Park
Ferry Terminal

Scale:

0 km   2 km   4 km

For more than a century there was confusion over Quadra's name. Named Valdes in honour of the Spanish explorer, three islands — present-day Quadra, Maurelle and Sonora — were thought to be one land mass. Later they were known as Valdes Islands. It wasn't until 1903 that it was completely sorted out and Quadra was renamed to differentiate it from Valdes Island in the southern Gulf Islands.

The island was named Quadra to commemorate the friendship between the English and Spanish explorers, Captain George Vancouver and Don Juan Francisco de la Bodega y Quadra. To please his friend, Vancouver had named the big island where they had met The Island of Quadra and Vancouver. Over the years the Quadra was dropped from use and it became simply Vancouver Island.

With its heavily indented shoreline and wooded slopes, Quadra is an exceptionally beautiful island. It has a network of lakes, long stretches of secluded shoreline with far-reaching views, and protected bays and coves. Off in the distance to east and north are the receding peaks of the islands of Desolation Sound and the mainland mountains. But along with the beauty there is danger.

To the west and east of Quadra are some of the most turbulent tidal rapids in British Columbia, Seymour and Surge narrows, where tidal streams can run up to 16 knots. The south end of the island is open to winds whipping up Georgia Strait, over about 65 kilometres of unimpeded water. This combination of constricted waterways and open fetches makes the waters around Quadra among the most dangerous on the coast. Travellers inadvisedly moving through the narrows on a large tidal exchange have reported huge whirlpools opening suddenly beneath them, and in

Quathiaski Cove.

some areas overfalls are common. Through ignorance, foolhardiness and bad luck, many lives and dozens of vessels have been lost.

It's hard to imagine when you see the tide rip through Seymour Narrows, but it is considerably safer today than it was several decades ago. Ripple Rock, in the centre of the channel and 3 metres below the surface at low tide, was the cause of deadly whirlpools and overfalls at full flood. Many ships foundered here, reportedly taking a total of 114 lives. For years, the idea of blowing Ripple Rock out of the water was discussed, but the first attempt, in 1942, ended in disaster when nine men going ashore from a drilling barge anchored over the rock were sucked into a whirlpool and drowned. In 1953, plans to tunnel underneath the rock from nearby Maud Island were revived, and on April 5, 1958, Ripple Rock was blasted out of the channel in the largest non-nuclear detonation recorded to that time.

Logging and mining brought the first settlers to Quadra and logging and fishing are the mainstays today. By island standards, Quadra bustles with industrious activity, its large well-provisioned supermarkets, well-maintained roads and handsome homes a measure of the island's prosperity.

Quadra is an island with something for everyone. It has protected waterways and tidal rapids, secluded stretches of beach and wilderness trails, as well as an active community life and lively pubs. You could easily spend a week or two on Quadra and not begin to exhaust its recreational possibilities.

Getting There

B.C. Ferries dock at Quathiaski Cove, a ten-minute ride from Campbell River. Check B.C. Ferries or the Travel Infocentre in Campbell River for ferry schedules. Check the telephone directory for airline service and water taxis to the island, as well as taxi service, and bicycle, canoe, kayak and small boat rentals. Local businesses can also provide information about the island.

A Route to Follow

The settled south tip of Quadra Island is serviced with good paved roads and includes many of the points of interest for a visitor to the island. The main route around the island is a loop that takes in much of this settled area.

A logical starting place is the ferry terminal at Quathiaski Cove, where commercial fishing and pleasure boats crowd the government docks and cottages cluster around the bay. This is one of the population centres on the island, and most of the commercial amenities can be found within a few blocks. Follow the road from the ferry past a complex of stores to where it joins Heriot Bay Road and turn right onto Heriot Bay Road. At the junction with West Road, turn left, following the signs to Heriot Bay and the Cortes Island ferry. It is about 6.5 kilometres from this junction to Heriot Bay. The island community centre is located on West Road at Blenkin Park. It incorporates the logging theme in its large log pillars, and the artistry of the islanders in its handcut fishscale shakes and stained glass windows. Blenkin Park is the start of a 1.3-kilometre walk that was the road between the old community hall (where the new one now stands) and Heriot Bay Road.

Within a few kilometres, West Road skirts Gowlland Harbour. The well-tended buildings, fences and pastures of Homewood lie between West Road and the harbour. Unfortunately, there is no public access to the harbour, although private resorts are located on the waterfront.

Homes and services, government docks, and private wharfs, as well as the ferry terminus for Cortes Island, are located at Heriot Bay. This is an interesting place to spend a few hours watching the comings and goings in the scenic and busy harbour, perhaps having some refreshment in the local pub and checking out the other facilities in the area. A small park with picnic tables on the waterfront near the Heriot Bay Inn makes an interesting stop for a picnic lunch, with views of Heriot Island and Open Bay and the Breton Islands in the distance.

From here, Heriot Bay Road follows along Drew Harbour. From the road you can see the long sandy arm of Rebecca Spit enclosing Drew Harbour. If you are enticed by the views, you can digress to one of Quadra's most beautiful areas, Rebecca Spit Provincial Park. To get to the park, turn left at Rebecca Spit Road, which runs along the head of Drew Harbour. The Cape Mudge Indian Band has established a commercial campground on their reserve land at the head of the harbour, abutting the provincial park.

There are large parking areas at the spit, as well as picnic tables, barbecue pits, pit toilets, drinking water and a launching ramp. There is no provincial campground.

It is no wonder that Rebecca Spit is one of the most popular destinations in summer. Currents can rage around Quadra's outer shores, but it is almost always calm within the protective arm of the spit. Often crowded in summer, it is quiet and almost magical in June and September, when you might share the area with only half a dozen other people and the many seashore birds.

To continue the route, return to Heriot Bay Road and go to the left. It is about 10 kilometres to the Cape Mudge Indian Village, but on the way you might want to detour to a beach access at the end of Smith Road. There is a parking area and a path to a pebble beach, studded with boulders and backed with tangled piles of bleached driftwood. Several unusual homes are visible from the road or the beach.

Approximately 7 kilometres from the junction with Rebecca Spit Road, Heriot Bay Road intersects with Cape Mudge Road. Turn left onto Cape Mudge Road, which leads through dense second-growth forest interspersed with occasional driveways and homes. The interesting signposts found here and along other roads on Quadra are peculiar to the island. Many local craftspeople and businesses are home-based, and a number of residents responded to the decision to assign street numbers to homeowner's lots by installing their own creative signposts. Local craftspeople have made many of the signs into works of art, but visitors must be forgiven for occasionally confusing the public and private signposts.

Watch for the turnoff to the Cape Mudge Indian Village and turn right on Weway Road. The village is located on the waterfront north of Cape Mudge. The museum here is well worth a visit: follow the signs to the south end of the village.

The Quadra Island United Church, near the museum, is a pretty white clapboard structure that dates from 1931. It was restored in the late 1970s, when the large stained-glass window with fishing imagery, designed by Russ Fuoco, was added. The church now serves all of Quadra. Inside the church, the whole east wall is made of carved yellow cedar designed by internationally-known artist Bill Reid and executed by carver Jim Hart, both from the Queen Charlotte Islands. The altar is covered with a button blanket cloth.

The Kwagiulth Museum and Cultural Centre is a tribute to the efforts

Innovative signposts are found along Quadra roads.

of native people of the coast, from Cape Mudge to Alert Bay, to repatriate their property and begin to retrieve their cultural heritage. Indian potlatches were banned by federal law in 1884, but it wasn't until the 1920s that this clash of European and native culture reached its peak. At that time, ceremonial headdresses, masks and coppers were confiscated and several people were jailed for failing to comply with the law. After years of negotiations, many of the belongings were returned, on condition that they

United Church in Cape Mudge village.

be housed in appropriate museums. The result was the establishment of the Kwagiulth Museum at Cape Mudge and the U'Mista Cultural Centre in Alert Bay. The history of the laws and the struggle for repatriation is described in more detail in the Cormorant Island chapter.

Opened in 1979, the Kwagiulth Museum houses masks, rattles, headdresses, coppers and other ceremonial objects. There is also a "hands-on" exhibit, where visitors can try on a ceremonial button blanket, watch a video, or make a crayon rubbing from a fibreglass casting of a petroglyph. The opening of the museum was appropriately celebrated with a huge potlatch and feast given by Chief Harry Assu of Cape Mudge, his son-in-law James Wilson, and Jim Sewid of Alert Bay.

Several granite boulders displaying petroglyphs are located in a waterfront park near the museum. The boulders were relocated from Cape Mudge in order to protect them from erosion and vandalism. Many more petroglyph boulders remain at Cape Mudge.

From the village it is possible to return to your starting point at Quathiaski Cove via Green Road, which skirts the shore before moving inland past Whiskey Point.

What the Main Route Misses

Cape Mudge and the Lighthouse

The gleaming white tower of the Cape Mudge lighthouse has been a warning beacon for mariners since it was established in 1898. Located at the southwest tip of Cape Mudge, it marks the treacherous waters over Wilby Shoals, a reef that extends for more than 3 kilometres south of the cape. The area is most dangerous when a southeast wind opposes a flood tide, creating overfalls and standing waves which can swamp even a large boat.

The passage between the lighthouse and Wilby Shoals is one of the favoured fishing areas for anglers from Quadra Island, Campbell River and surrounding areas. The water here is often choked with boats, from 4-metre recreational runabouts to large commercial trollers.

To get to the lighthouse, take Cape Mudge Road, turn right onto Joyce Road, then right again onto Lighthouse Road. Park beside the lighthouse. You can hike the beach in front of the lighthouse, but this land is Indian Reserve, and to walk here without permission means you could be trespassing.

A beach walk around the cape can be fascinating at low tide. Large granite boulders scattered near the high tide line bear dozens of petroglyphs, some hardly visible. Wear comfortable shoes, as the large rounded rocks are hard to walk on. At the tip of the cape are 60-metre-high sand cliffs that can be seen for miles. It was here, in 1792, that Captain Vancouver rowed ashore and met the residents of a Salish village located at the top of the cliffs. Archibald Menzies, the ship's botanist, estimated the village to be inhabited by 350 people, housed in 12 buildings. This strategic site was later taken over by the warlike Lekwiltok band of the Kwakiutl Indians, in about 1850.

Francisco Point

To get to Francisco Point, take Cape Mudge Road to its end, to where the road forks. Francisco Point is to the left. A short spur, Petroglyph Road, gives access to Dogfish Bay and Francisco Point on the southeast side of the island.

Backing the pebble beach are tangles of weathered logs and piles of bleached and broken sticks. The large granite boulders may reveal petroglyphs to the keen observer if the light is right, but the petroglyphs have been severely eroded and are difficult to make out. There are views of Cortes and Marina islands from Dogfish Bay. As you round the point, there are sweeping views to the south.

Quadra Island Salmon Hatchery

Unlike most Gulf Islands, Quadra has many salmon-bearing streams. The Quadra Island Salmon Enhancement Society was established to preserve and rebuild salmon stocks. Its facilities, scattered over several sites, include a fish hatchery, spawning channels, fish traps, and a lake pen in which fry are reared. The society has successfully restocked

Cape Mudge lighthouse.

Drew Creek, which had no salmon more than a decade ago, as well as Hyacinthe Creek and the Village Bay Lake system.

The hatchery, which has incubation equipment, a brood stock holding area and fry-rearing troughs, is open to the public, but personnel are often out in the field. In summer the hatchery is usually closed due to low water levels.

To get there, take West Road and turn left onto Hyacinthe Bay Road. The hatchery is signposted.

Lucky Jim Mine

The Lucky Jim Mine is the relic of a mining operation that at its height is said to have removed 1,100 tonnes of gold and copper ore a month from several shafts. The mine operated from 1903 to 1910. All that remains today are a few ghostly reminders: a huge iron flywheel, the covered pits of the shafts and some deteriorating signs. On the way in, about half a dozen log cabins — the original bunkhouses of the mine workers — are subsiding slowly back into the forest.

To get to the mine site, take the Granite Bay Road turnoff. After about 6 kilometres, the road makes a sharp turn to the left. The road to the mine joins Granite Bay Road in a T here. It is a somewhat rough, overgrown road, but passable to most vehicles. You can park at the roadside and walk in for less than half a kilometre. Take the first left fork in the road, then the middle trail when the road splits into three.

Remains of the Lucky Jim Mine.

Emergencies and Information

Quadra Island has its own RCMP detachment. Check the telephone directory for the phone number and address of the island medical clinic. The nearest hospital is in Campbell River. Emergency numbers are at the front of the telephone directory, or the operator can likely assist you.

The Campbell River Infocentre or the Campbell River Chamber of Commerce can provide information on Quadra Island. Local businesses have maps and publications about the island. For information on new hiking trails, you can try asking at the community centre — the Quadra Island Recreation Society is housed there and is involved in developing trails on the island.

Camping and Accommodation

There are no provincial campgrounds on Quadra, but the Cape Mudge Indian Band operates a campground near Rebecca Spit. There are 140 well-treed oceanfront and forest campsites. Showers and flush toilets are available. Some of the resorts on Quadra Island may also have camping facilities.

For more information on campgrounds, resorts, lodges, hotels, motels, and bed and breakfast establishments or other accommodation, refer to Tourism B.C.'s *Accommodations* booklet, described in Chapter One.

Shopping and Services

Two shopping areas on Quadra, located near Quathiaski Cove and Heriot Bay, include well-stocked grocery stores, post offices, liquor outlets, and craft and antique stores. Quadra also has restaurants and pubs, gas station and car repairs, marinas, churches and many more services.

The community centre is a focal point of island culture, organizing events that draw on local and outside talent.

Recreation and Events

Check with the Campbell River Infocentre or local businesses for information on canoe, kayak or bicycle rentals, horseback riding, nature tours and scenic, diving or fishing charters. There are tennis courts at Blenkin Park. In the winter, island residents can sometimes enjoy cross-country skiing and skating on small lakes and ponds.

Quadra Island has been holding an annual May Day celebration since the first years of settlement. Held at the end of May at Rebecca Spit, it features parades, competitions, selection of a May Queen, a regatta and more. Other annual celebrations include a June salmon barbecue.

Hiking — Wilderness Trails

The north end of Quadra is honeycombed with old logging roads, many dating from the early years of this century. Some of the locals are familiar with these trails and may be able to give you information on trailheads and routes. However, there are several well-marked trails of varying degrees of difficulty that are more easily accessible to the traveller.

Quadra is fortunate in having an active community group, the Quadra Island Recreation Society, which has built and maintains a number of trails on the island, in conjunction with forestry companies holding tree farm licences. Four major trails are completed, and others are in the planning stages.

Morte Lake Trail

Morte Lake is a popular swimming spot. The water is clear and warm and there is a sandy beach at its eastern end. The hike to the lake, with time for a picnic lunch and a refreshing swim, can nicely occupy a half day or more.

The head of the Morte Lake Trail is located .7 kilometre down Walcan (Missing Links) Road, on the right side. There is a grassy parking area and an information shelter with a map of the area, including all the trails. The trail to the lake begins on a logging road that passes through an alder grove, then enters tall second-growth forest, with an understory of ferns, Oregon grape, salal, huckleberry and lacy young fir. Along the trail are signs of early logging — huge stumps with springboard notches, and old skid roads. The trail passes Little Morte Lake, and several steep rock outcroppings to the right, before descending to the lake. Here it splits and you can choose between the north route, which circumnavigates the lake, or the south loop. The south loop connects with the north loop at the marshy south tip of the lake, then proceeds south, leading through a marshy area behind Mud Lake, then along Walcan Road to the parking area. The north trail leads steeply uphill and affords lovely views of the lake and surrounding forest, with the peaks of Vancouver Island in the far distance.

The trail is generally easy going, with a few steep portions. The south loop, 7.2 kilometres, can be hiked in about two hours. The north loop around the top of the lake, another 3 kilometres, will probably add an hour to the hike.

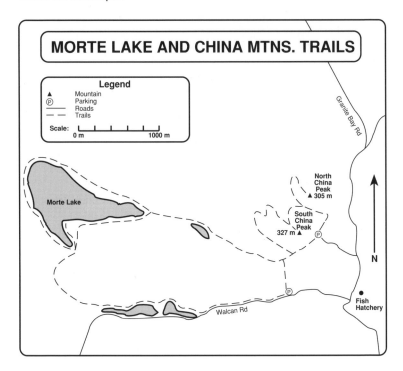

China Mountains

From the China Mountain peaks there are spectacular panoramic views of the passages and islands surrounding Quadra and the distant peaks of the Coast Mountains on the mainland. South and North China Mountains can be hiked in a loop trail, or separate trails followed to each of the peaks. South China Mountain, the higher of the two peaks at 327 metres, has a somewhat better view.

The trailhead is located just past the salmon hatchery on Hyacinthe Bay Road. Watch for a roadside sign to your left. At the parking area, there is a large signboard with a map of the trails. (You can also reach the China Mountains trail via a connector from the Morte Lake trail; the connector is marked on both trailhead maps.) All forks are marked with either posted signs or cairns.

The trail, which begins innocently enough as a gentle incline on an old logging road, becomes quite strenuous as it ascends, leading steeply uphill and along narrow paths around rocky outcroppings. However, viewpoints on bluffs as you ascend give a taste of the views to come, and there are more level areas through woods where you can catch your breath. Don't be surprised if you flush several grouse through the woodlands. From the bluffs, eagles and turkey vultures are often spotted.

The views at the top are worth the effort of getting there. From the mossy knoll at the peak, you can see the south end of Quadra far below, with Read, Maurelle, and Cortes islands and the mountains of the mainland receding into the far distance. To the west are Campbell River and Discovery Passage, backed by the Vancouver Island ranges.

The trail to South China Peak is about 1.5 kilometres one way; round trip takes about an hour. The loop trail encompassing both peaks is 3.5 kilometres.

Newton Lake Trail

The Newton Lake trail takes you past five lakes, through damp, lush, overgrown forest, raw clearcut, and mature second growth forest with an open understory.

To get there, take Granite Bay Road to within a few hundred metres of Granite Bay. Turn right at the sign for Newton Lake Trail. About 700 metres along, there is a parking area for the trail. The first part of the trail climbs at a slow steady rate, then it levels out. The three lakes on the route to Newton Lake are all small; one is little more than a swamp. The still waters are covered with lily pads and broken with the jagged snags of sunken trees. Woodpeckers and jays are frequently sighted among the trees and herons fish at the marshy edges of the lakes.

View of Rebecca Spit from South China Mountain.

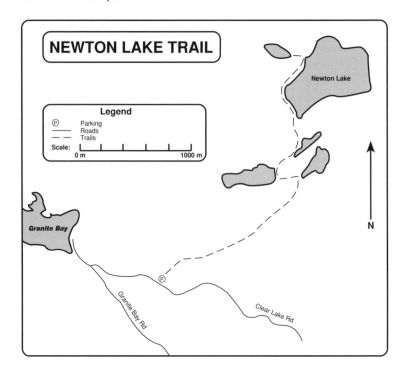

Newton Lake is jewellike when it is calm. Its waters are a strange deep teal green and it is heavily treed to the shoreline. The path leads around the western edge of the lake through an open forest of firs. The spongy forest floor is carpeted with fir and pine needles and moss. For many hikers, the large rock outcropping on the northwest shore of the lake is a destination. The flat, mossy knoll makes a good site for a picnic lunch and a swim. Children and others might amuse themselves by playing with the echo produced from the north end of the lake.

The trail is wide and well-marked and can be hiked in an hour or so, one way.

Nugedzi Lake Old-Growth Forest Trail

A new trail developed near Mount Seymour takes in a variety of environments, but it is most notable because it allows a rare opportunity to enjoy old-growth forest.

The entrance to the trail is about 2.5 kilometres past the salmon hatchery on Hyacinthe Bay Road, where there is a rough road to the left with a parking area. Perhaps half a kilometre farther down this old logging road, a trail leads off to the old-growth forest. An easy, marked, walking trail, about 5 kilometres in length, winds among large trees with an open,

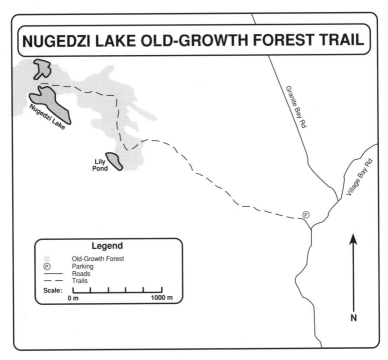

NUGEDZI LAKE OLD-GROWTH FOREST TRAIL

Nugedzi Lake

Lily Pond

Granite Bay Rd

Village Bay Rd

P

Legend

Old-Growth Forest
P Parking
—— Roads
– – Trails
Scale: |___|___|___|___|___|
0 m   1000 m

N

mossy understory. Boardwalks have been constructed through the swampy areas. The trail is a fairly steady up-hill climb, which levels out once it enters the old-growth forest.

Rebecca Spit

Rebecca Spit is a 2-kilometre-long, narrow neck of land that forms the eastern arm of Drew Harbour. In 1959 it was officially established as a park, when the land was acquired from the Clendenings, who originally had a homestead at the entrance to the spit. The park comprises 175 hectares and facilities include trails, picnic areas with tables and firepits, and a boat launch ramp.

The trails at Rebecca Spit provide easy, level walking on excellent pathways. Start just inside the park gates, and follow along the road to the parking lot. Trails lead along both sides of the spit, joining to form one trail at its narrowest points.

At no point is the spit wider than about 100 metres, but the inner and outer edges are quite different. By taking advantage of the trails, it's possible to enjoy both perspectives.

The protected water of Drew Harbour attracts a wide variety of waterbirds, including loons, harlequin ducks, and herons. On the outer edge, there are views across to Cortes and Marina islands and the mainland mountains. Grassy areas are interspersed with wooded sections with large trees and an understory of ferns, salal and Oregon grape.

Near the tip of the spit, fireweed adds a bright glow to the silvery trunks of a stand of dead trees. An earthquake in 1946, measuring 7.2 on the Richter scale, caused the land here to sink, killing the trees and reducing the spit by about 1.2 hectares.

The entire walk covers approximately 4 kilometres and can be done in about an hour. However, most people want to spend much longer here, enjoying the views, beachcombing along the outside edge or simply watching the passage of birds and boats.

Sunrise and sunset are particularly nice at Rebecca Spit. On a September morning, the sun comes up over the ridge around 8:30, dispelling the remaining wisps of mist over the mirror-smooth waters of Drew Harbour. Gulls pick over the leavings of the tide as it begins to ebb, and loons call across the water, their cries lingering on the still air. In the nearby Douglas firs, dozens of crows caucus noisily, leaving in a flurry as a larger raven draws near, its powerful wings parting the air with a silken sound. On the

Newton Lake.

beach, a great blue heron scours the shore in slow motion. Its morning routine could take two or three hours, yet it may cover only 50 metres of shoreline. As the early-rising anglers put in to shore, the second shift prepares to launch their boats.

Paddling and Small Boating — Ocean and Freshwater Routes

Quadra Island is a paradise for paddlers. Gowlland and Drew harbours and the Main Lake Chain provide excellent sheltered paddling in most conditions. For the more experienced paddler or small boater, there are also some exciting trips in the channels and coves around the island. However — and this cannot be emphasized too strongly — these waters can be deadly for the novice or for those who do not study local tides and currents. If the situation is not dangerous, it is at the very least inconvenient to be swept several kilometers past your destination and have to wait hours for a tide change to get back. Even in relatively protected waters, the wise (or lazy) paddler will plan a trip to make use of tidal streams to conserve energy. The following trips are suitable for most paddlers. An ability to read current and tide charts, and local knowledge, is required for most of the water around Quadra.

Main Lake Chain

Distance: variable. *Launching*: Village Bay Lake or Mine Lake.

If you want a peaceful paddle in sheltered conditions, without having to worry about times and tides, the Main Lake Chain is for you. This interconnecting network of lakes is the largest freshwater waterway in the Gulf or Discovery islands. The lakes offer paddling on placid waters, an everchanging shoreline, pretty beaches and islands, and good trout fishing. Except for Village Bay Lake, the shores are sparsely settled and wildlife is abundant. Loons and other water birds, kingfishers, eagles, deer and otters can all be seen near the lakes.

To get to the lakes, take Village Bay Road. It is sometimes steep, with loose gravel in places, but passable for most vehicles. At the bridge that crosses the narrows of Village Bay Lake, there is a parking lot and a good boat launching area. Dozens of small aluminum boats belonging to residents will tell you you're in the right place. From here you can paddle under the bridge and to the north end of Village Bay Lake.

After the cluster of cottages near the bridge, habitations are few. Along the shore, mossy, treeless bluffs are interspersed with shallow lagoons, where reedy grasses and water lilies grow in abundance. Watch for two

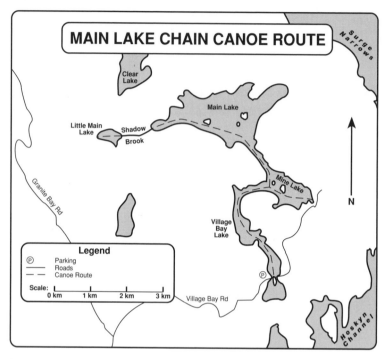

huge eagle nests high in the trees on the western shore of the first lake.

The channel connecting Village Bay and Mine lakes is a shallow, winding, reed-choked passage known by locals as "the gut." At the exit to Mine Lake, the hulks of huge logs loom up from the lake bottom. A somewhat eery sight, they are reminders that the lakes were once booming grounds when the system was used to transport huge logs cut from the original forests of this entire area. In 1894, the Hastings Sawmill Company dammed the outlet to raise the level of the lakes through the shallows. The logs were taken out to the head of Village Bay, where a trail now exists.

Mine Lake has some inviting little islands. After entering Mine Lake, paddle to the farthest island to the right (if you go to the left, you will get to Main Lake), where there is a tiny sandy beach, just large enough to land a canoe, and a campsite on its southeast end. Rock slabs are sheltered by an open forest of fir and pine and the flat rocks, carpeted in soft pine needles and moss, are like large outdoor rooms.

The Narrows is the passage connecting Main and Mine lakes. A couple of sandy beaches on the eastern shore of the passage are good places to stop for a swim, a picnic, or an overnight stay. The signs of previous campers — fire pits, rough table arrangements and benches — may be visible.

Main Lake, the largest of the chain, is exceptionally pretty, with bays and several islands to explore. You can spend an afternoon exploring this lake, or you may want to complete the chain with Little Main Lake. To get there, follow along the south shore to a narrow opening at the westernmost tip of the lake. Shadow Brook is a picturesque channel providing canoes and kayaks access to Little Main Lake for most of the year. Quiet, peaceful and enclosed, it winds among high reeds and water lilies. In midsummer, you may have to portage or pull your craft through the shallowest spots.

To launch at Mine Lake, bypassing Village Bay Lake and the shallows between it and Mine Lake, go past the bridge over Village Bay Lake, and turn left onto Surge Narrows Road. About 2.4 kilometres from the turnoff is a launching area on Mine Lake.

Canoeing the narrow passage between Village Bay and Mine lakes.

Rebecca Spit and Drew Harbour

Distance: variable. *Launching*: Rebecca Spit.

Drew Harbour is one of the more sheltered ocean paddling areas around Quadra Island and is a great place for kids to explore in a dinghy on calm summer days. If the weather is calm, you can explore the outside of the spit, or cross to Heriot Bay.

Gowlland Harbour

Distance: variable. *Launching*: ask permission at marine ways on Anderson Road.

Gowlland Harbour is one of the prettiest harbours in the area and is worth the effort of asking if you can launch here. There is no public access to the water, but you may be able to get permission to launch a canoe or kayak from Phillips Marine on Anderson Road or from one of a number of marinas and resorts on the waterfront.

Gowlland Harbour is well protected from the rapid tidal stream just outside the entrance by Gowlland Island. Currents can be swift over the shallow waters between April Point and Gowlland Island, so this is an area to be avoided.

Several small islands and rocky islets dot the harbour. These islands, which are covered with wildflowers in the spring, are protected in a provincial park reserve. Harbour seals in the dozens congregate here, and are not shy about investigating paddlers.

Granite Bay to Small Inlet

Distance: 12 nautical miles return. *Launching*: Granite Bay.

The road to the boat launch at Granite Bay is very rough, so you may have to portage your canoe or kayak to the water if your vehicle is not a four-wheel drive. Granite Bay is an interesting paddle in a remote area with an intriguing history of use.

The area immediately around Granite Bay, now occupied by a handful of people, was once a thriving village of more than 500 people. Evidence of logging, farming and mining activities from around the turn of the century can still be found along the shores. Several fish farms have now become established in the area.

Hug the shoreline to your right as you come out of Granite Bay. Once through the narrow, shallow entrance to Small Inlet, there is complete protection from wind and tides. An 800-metre trail leads from the head of the inlet to Waiatt Bay on the west side of Quadra. The path is on private land, but you may be able to get permission to use it. Energetic paddlers with knowledge of tidal currents might want to portage their craft to Waiatt Bay and investigate the Octopus Islands, a 109-hectare marine park at the head of the bay. Here care must be taken, as eddies and tidal currents extend down from Hole in the Wall and the Upper Rapids of Okisollo Channel.

Heriot Bay to Open Bay

Distance: 10 nautical miles return. *Launching*: Heriot Bay.

The convoluted coastline from Heriot Bay to Open Bay is an interesting day trip. Once out of busy Heriot Bay, where paddlers must exercise caution in avoiding the Cortes Island ferry and other marine traffic, you can peacefully explore the many nooks and crannies of Hyacinthe Bay and Open Bay. Open Bay consists of four small bays with sandy beaches. See the section titled The Land — Rain Forests, Grasslands and Wildflowers, in Chapter One, for a description of unusual rock formations at Open Bay. Some of the shore on Hyacinthe Point, on the southwest side of Open Bay, and an island just outside the bay, north of the Breton Islands, make up a provincial park reserve. They are undeveloped, but are set aside for recreational use.

If wind and tide permit, you could venture out to the Breton Islands. Sea lions and eagles may congregate in the passage between Quadra and these islands in early spring.

When You Arrive by Private Boat

Quathiaski Cove

Quathiaski Cove has a government dock, but the terminus for the ferry to Quadra from Vancouver Island is nearby, so it is subject to frequent ferry wash. Up the hill from the ferry are all the amenities, including food stores, post office, liquor outlet, restaurants and other commercial outlets. A pub by the ferry terminal is a popular gathering spot.

Heriot Bay

Heriot Bay is often crowded and busy, with the ferry terminal for Cortes Island, government floats and marinas. The government floats are usually crowded, especially in the summer, but space may be available at the marinas. Anchoring is possible in Heriot Bay, as well as Hyacinthe and Open bays to the north, but all are open to infrequent summer southeasters.

Gas, groceries, and other supplies are available nearby. There are crafts outlets, a pub and restaurants.

Village Bay

Fairly protected anchorage is available in the southwest corner of Village Bay, named for the large Indian village that once occupied the bay: it is marked by a small reserve at the northern cove. From this cove, it is a short, 400-metre hike to Village Bay Lake, the first in the Main Lake Chain. This waterway is described in Paddling and Small Boating, in this chapter.

Rebecca Spit Provincial Marine Park

In summer, there is usually a collection of boats in the lee of Rebecca Spit. The best place is just inside the tip, where the hook forms a shallow curve. The spit is a lovely place to explore on foot, although it can be crowded in the summer. All amenities are available nearby at Heriot Bay, about an hour's walk away.

The beach at Drew Harbour.

Octopus Islands Provincial Marine Park

Good all-weather anchorage is available in Waiatt Bay, but it can be crowded, as it is a popular stop before venturing north through the Upper Rapids or Hole in the Wall. Octopus Islands Marine Park, at the entrance to the bay, occupies 109 hectares comprising some of the small islands and islets (the two largest are privately owned) and the upland behind the small bay at the north end of Waiatt Bay. An 800-metre trail connects the head of Waiatt Bay to Small Inlet on the east side of Quadra. The trail is on private property, but you may be able to get permission to use it.

Kanish Bay

The inner waters of Kanish Bay, Granite Bay at its southwest end, and Small Inlet provide protected anchorage in all weather. The area is interesting because it was once a busy logging and mining community which has all but disappeared. Over the last several years, several fish farms have operated in this area.

Quadra Fishing

The fishing around Quadra is thought by many to be the best on the coast, and Quadra has all the facilities an angler could want, including a variety of guided fishing charters. As with other water sports in this area, it is essential that anglers who venture out in their own boats know how to read tide and current tables and have specific local knowledge.

A line cast into the water almost anywhere around Quadra could yield a catch, but a number of hot spots attract anglers in search of the big chinooks that gather here in August and September. Some are angling for a place in Campbell River's Tyee Club. Tyee is an Indian word meaning "chief" or "king," and these chinook, weighing in at 13.6 kilograms (30 pounds) or more — up to 32 kilograms — are certainly the best of their species. The Tyee Club was founded in 1924 and has specific rules governing membership. Among other regulations, anglers must declare their intention to try for a tyee, they must use a rod of a specific length, line tested for 20-pound breaking strength, and an artificial lure, and they must troll from a rowboat or other non-motorized craft. This last regulation means that sheltered water is required, and many anglers head for the Campbell River estuary.

Fishing around Quadra is a year-round activity, depending on the weather. May brings the bluebacks to Discovery Passage; chinooks arrive in June and July, with the big salmon in August and September.

Cape Mudge Lighthouse and Wilby Shoals

Launching: Quathiaski Cove.

Even on a calm day, the waters race past Cape Mudge. The current, which runs at up to 7 knots, and the extensive shoals off the cape cause a back eddy that is a favourite haunt for anglers. They congregate opposite the lighthouse, drifting with the current and then taking advantage of the back eddy to return to their starting point. At prime times, the water is almost obscured by boats, from aluminum runabouts to commercial trollers. Wilby Shoals are fished from close in to the sand cliffs to up to 3 kilometres from shore.

The water here is productive year-round, with excellent fishing for coho in summer. Fishing for chinooks is good all year and greenling, lingcod and rockcod are caught in winter. However, strong winds keep most anglers away from Wilby Shoals in winter, when dangerous rips are formed by prevailing southeasterlies opposing the flood tide. Even in summer, winds can spring up suddenly, and anglers should keep a close watch on the weather.

Copper Bluffs

Launching: Quathiaski Cove.

Around the beginning of August, the tyee seem to congregate around Copper Bluffs. Anglers fish tight in to the cliffs because of the big dropoff. Currents are fast and dangerous here.

April Point

Launching: Quathiaski Cove.

One of the longest-established fishing lodges on the coast is located at April Point, a testament to the good fishing here. April Point intrudes into the fast-moving currents of Discovery Passage, creating a back eddy. Salmon move into the harbour with bait fish and tides. Coho congregate here from May or June; the big northern cohoes arrive in late September. Greenling, lingcod and rockfish are caught along the dropoffs.

Hazards include navigation of the shallows at the south entrance to the harbour and fast-moving currents at both entrances.

Quathiaski Cove

Launching: Quathiaski Cove.

Quathiaski Cove is a busy harbour, but it can be a productive fishing area, particularly around the entrances to the cove north and south of

Grouse Island, where currents are constantly moving. Anglers must take care to stay out of the path of the ferry travelling to and from Vancouver Island. Chinooks up to 3 kilograms are caught all winter, and big chinooks and coho in August to September. The back eddies at Whiskey Point can also be productive.

Main Lake Chain

Launching: Village Bay Lake or Mine Lake.

There is a substantial population of cutthroat trout in these lakes, with an average size of 35 to 40 centimetres. A trout derby has been an annual event for some years.

Quadra Scuba Diving

Some of the best — and most challenging — scuba-diving territory in the world is off the shores of Quadra Island. Divers flock here all year round, attracted by the wide array of life that flourishes in the cold, clear, constantly changing waters of the tidal channels. In some places the underwater surfaces are completely covered with a riot of colour: the bright pink of strawberry anemones, iridescent algae and a variety of sponges and starfish — a fantasy for macrophotographers.

However, this water is not for the novice. The factor that probably contributes most to the proliferation of underwater life — the rapid, ever-changing water — limits most of the dives to the expert category. All divers should familiarize themselves with diving in cold water and rapid currents, and they must have an experienced person who knows the area in a surface boat. These waters are *dangerous*, and must be respected.

In Discovery Passage, the area bounded by the shores of Quadra to the east, Seymour Narrows to the north, and a diagonal line drawn from the government dock in Campbell River to Cape Mudge is closed to removal of marine life by divers. For exact boundaries, check Fisheries guidelines.

Check local listings for diving companies which provide services, including accommodation. It is wise to book ahead during busy seasons, as accommodations on the island are somewhat limited. Air is available on the island.

Seymour Narrows

Boat dive. Launching: Quathiaski Cove.

All of Seymour Narrows provides good diving. Close to the Vancouver Island shore, at a depth of about 18 to 21 metres, there is the most variety and density of marine life. It is a spectacular, colourful dive with strawberry anemones, sponges, nudibranchs, tubeworms and giant barnacles. Puget Sound king crabs, kelp greenlings, rockfish and dogfish hide in the crevices.

Dives here are short: the tide is slack for only 15 to 20 minutes, and even then there is considerable movement. The escort boat should be large and powerful enough to withstand the current, and the operator should be experienced in the area.

Copper Cliffs

Boat dive. Launching: Quathiaski Cove.

Situated at the north end of Gowlland Harbour, the cliffs rise vertically from the water for 90 metres. Scoured by the current, the underwater wall is flat and sheer with few crevices. At depths of about 24 to 48 metres, the wall is covered with colourful, small, low-profile marine life — rock scallops, crimson anemones and an abundance of sponges and featherduster tubeworms. Nearby May Island is a good second dive because it is shallow and usually free of currents. Puget Sound king crabs are sometimes found in large numbers here, near a wreck off the north tip of the island.

Needless to say, Copper Cliffs must be attempted only at slack tide and there must be an experienced person in a surface boat. Anglers fishing close up to the cliffs can be a hazard: ascend as close as possible to the wall.

Steep Island

Boat dive. Launching: Quathiaski Cove.

The north tip of Steep Island in Gowlland Harbour is noted for the variety of sponges and tubeworms that thrive there, particularly the gigantic featherduster tubeworms — possibly the most spectacular in all the coastal waters — which are found at 21 metres or more. At around 33 metres there is an overhanging ledge that is covered with soft yellow sponges, red sponges and red soft coral.

Friendly seals live around Gowlland Island. Sometimes dozens hang out near the log booms on the east side of the island. They often swim with divers, who snorkel and float with the seals. The seals have become so tame they will eat from a diver's hand and allow themselves to be touched.

April Point

Boat dive. Launching: Quathiaski Cove.

April Point is ideal territory for macrophotography. It has a wealth of small, colourful life and is particularly noted for the abundance of carpeting strawberry anemones. Wolf eels can be spied in the cracks and ledges as you descend along the wall past the dropoff. This is a 35- to 40-minute dive, maximum, because of tidal currents. A boat with a depth sounder is required for this dive, as the dropoff is quite far from shore.

Quathiaski Cove

Shore dive. Walk in from the old ferry landing or enter from the government wharf.

This easy dive is good at night, because of the nocturnal creatures found here. There is plenty of life right at the dock: tubeworms and sponges can be seen on pilings and hanging from the wharf. There are nudibranchs and sponges, as well as kelp greenlings, dogfish, penpoint gunnels, sailfin sculpins and octopi.

Whiskey Point

Boat dive. Launching: Quathiaski Cove.

The rocky ledges at Whiskey Point are covered in colourful anemones, algae and sponges. Shellfish, lingcod and kelp greenlings are common, and the area is noted for its friendly rockfish and tame wolf-eels that eat from your hand. At the base of the wall off the point, there is a small ledge

Wolf-eel.

at a depth of about 15 metres. A boulder on the ledge is the home of a wolf eel dubbed Captain Crunch by divers. About 1.6 metres long, Captain Crunch emerges to greet divers and reportedly enjoys being held and touched.

Dive only at slack tide. Although you can make this dive from shore, most divers, even when entering from shore, will want to have a companion in a boat nearby.

Surge Narrows

Boat dive. Launching: Rebecca Spit.

Surge Narrows is similar to Seymour Narrows, with currents running up to 12 knots. The water here is never still, even at slack tide. At depths of about 21 metres, there are anemones and fields of densely packed featherduster tubeworms that undulate with the current. Every spot in the narrows has something growing or living. There are surprises in the cracks and crevices: check out empty barnacle cases, which sometimes harbour two crabs.

Dives are limited to a short slack tide, as the current never really stops. Divers must be accompanied by a boat operated by someone with experience in the area.

Rebecca Spit

Shore dive.

This is a safe dive for all levels of experience, and you don't have to wait for tides. Near a ledge that drops to about 12 metres, there is a variety of life, from crabs to ling cod.

Cortes Island

Off the Tourist Track

 The difference between Quadra and Cortes islands is obvious the minute you drive off the ferry in Whaletown Bay. The quiet cove slumbers in the sun, a few boats sloshing at anchor from the ferry wash. When the cars disperse and the ferry departs, intense quiet returns, the only sounds the wind in the trees surrounding the bay, or occasional voices from across the cove.

The 45-minute crossing from Quadra has a profound impact on the nature of Cortes Island — a quiet, remote island with few settlements, scattered homes, and a beautiful coastline shared only by the wildlife and other human wanderers.

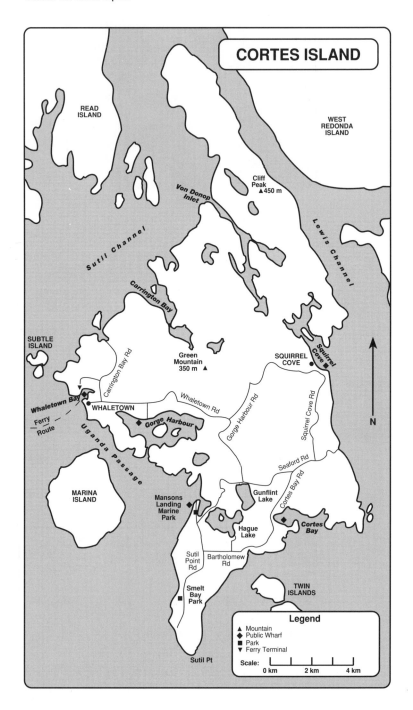

CORTES ISLAND

READ ISLAND

WEST REDONDA ISLAND

Cliff Peak ▲450 m

Von Donop Inlet

Sutil Channel

Lewis Channel

Carrington Bay

SUBTLE ISLAND

Green Mountain 350 m ▲

SQUIRREL COVE

Squirrel Cove

Carrington Bay Rd

Whaletown Bay

WHALETOWN

Gorge Harbour Rd

Squirrel Cove Rd

N

Whaletown Rd

♦ Gorge Harbour

Ferry Route

Uganda Passage

Seaford Rd

MARINA ISLAND

Mansons Landing Marine Park

Gunflint Lake

Cortes Bay Rd

Hague Lake

♦ Cortes Bay

Sutil Point Rd

Bartholomew Rd

TWIN ISLANDS

Smelt Bay Park ■

Legend
▲ Mountain
♦ Public Wharf
■ Park
▼ Ferry Terminal

Scale:
0 km   2 km   4 km

Sutil Pt

A hundred years ago, Cortes was much like other islands — remote, yet full of possibilities. Entrepreneurs saw it as a land of promise, surveying the tracts of virgin timber, schooling fish, abundant wildlife and underground mineral potential.

The first industry on Cortes was whaling. Today the only whales seen regularly in the inland passages are killer whales, but humpbacks were once abundant in Georgia Strait. In his journal of 1792, Captain George Vancouver noted large numbers playing in the waters around his ship. From 1869, Whaletown Bay was the site of a processing plant for whales caught in Georgia Strait, and thousands of litres of whale oil were exported. Soon, however, the whales were seriously depleted, and by 1870 the whaling station was closed.

Miners and loggers came to Cortes and left again, perhaps defeated by the isolation. Around the turn of the century, the Department of Lands enticed settlers to preempt land in the unsettled north by issuing booklets that touted the equable climate, "soil unsurpassed" for farming, ready markets for produce, and good steamboat service from the Union Steamship Company. By this time, around 1915, farmers and hand loggers had settled at Mansons Landing and Whaletown, and Cortes was one of the most populated islands in the northern group.

Over the years populations have fluctuated and development has come and gone, driven by local and worldwide economies. The island population has stabilized at just over 600, concentrated at the south end. The north end is a wilderness crisscrossed with trails and old logging roads and dotted with lakes. Much of its timber was logged around the turn of the century and over the following decades. Today Cortes, like many areas in B.C., is undergoing a transition phase as the mature second-growth forest is once again ready for logging. The community has made concerted efforts to preserve areas in the north, long used by locals as recreational areas. With increasing pressure on all the Gulf Islands for recreational property, it is hoped that residents of Cortes can monitor development in the future, sorting out the difficult issues of conservation, recreational potential and economics.

One of the most scenic of the islands, Cortes has an intricate coastline with protected waters for paddling and anchoring. While there has been talk over the years of developing its tourism potential, the island has a unique, quiet charm that is valued by both residents and visitors, many of whom would not like to see it change much.

Getting There

The ferry terminal on Cortes is at Whaletown Bay, a 45-minute trip from Heriot Bay on Quadra Island. Check at the Infocentre in Campbell

River or with B.C. Ferries for the schedule. Local businesses and marinas can provide information on boat rentals on the island. There may be a local transportation service with scheduled stops in Campbell River, Quadra Island and Cortes.

A Route to Follow

From the ferry terminal at Whaletown Bay, it is possible to take a more or less circular route around the settled southern end of Cortes Island. After disembarking from the ferry, follow the main road, which leads around the head of the bay. Bear right at Carrington Bay Road, just after a sign listing various establishments on the island.

At the junction with Whaletown Road, take the 1-kilometre detour to Whaletown, where the General Store, what may well be the world's tiniest freestanding post office, the Louisa Tooker Library and several homes perch on the south shores of the bay. The church, a plain, pretty structure, was built in 1951, part of the Anglican church's Columbia Coast Mission founded in 1905. A little bit of England has found its way to Cortes Island via the General Store. British street signs decorate the wharf and the garden has an air of English country. Travellers can check out the notice board at the store, which may provide information about the island.

Return along Whaletown Road, which twists and winds around the protected shores of Gorge Harbour. Public access to Gorge Harbour is via Hunt and Robertson roads, where there is a marina and a government wharf. Past the harbour, the road splits; bear right on Gorge Harbour Road, following the signs to Mansons Landing. After a few kilometres of travel through a forested area, there is an intersection with Seaford Road. Turn right, following signposts for Mansons Landing Provincial Marine Park, past Gunflint Lake and an idyllic farm where deer often browse along with the horses and cattle. To take a short detour into the park, turn right at Sutil Point Road.

Mansons Landing, named after Michael Manson who settled there in 1886, was one of the first areas of Cortes to be settled. Manson operated a successful trading post, swapping supplies for dogfish oil with native Indians and selling the oil as a lubricant to the mines in Nanaimo. Manson was a colourful character who became Justice of the Peace for Cortes and surrounding islands, later moving to Comox to work as superintendent in the Wellington Collieries and serving two terms as a member of the legislature, 1909 to 1912 and 1928 to 1932. Manson's brother John stayed on Cortes, selling meat to remote northern lumber camps and as far south as Comox, using a rowboat for transportation. By 1916, Mansons Landing had a cooperative store, post office, telegraph office and school.

Mansons Landing Provincial Marine Park was established in 1974. It occupies 100 hectares and encompasses seashore and lagoon areas as well as shoreline on Hague Lake. A store and government wharf are located here. The park has an interesting combination of features: beautiful white sand beaches, a protected lagoon, shellfish and a forested path to parkland on Hague Lake.

To get back on the route, return to Sutil Point Road and continue south, following signs to Smelt Bay. The community hall is located along this road. The centre is a focal point of island life and has facilities for residents, including the North Island Community College, a post office, a cafe and other amenities.

At the junction with Bartholomew Road, bear left, following the signs to Cortes Bay. The road climbs, then descends to the bay, passing scattered farm sites. A short road just before you get to the bay leads to the government wharf at Cortes Bay. From the wharf you can see most of the bay.

Cortes Island post office.

The main road continues along the bay. A short distance past the bay watch for Manzanita Road. A detour down this road will reveal the surprising sight of turrets rising above the dense forest, surmounted by a flag pole flying the Canadian flag. An enterprising islander has built a five-storey castle here, out of cement blocks and ingenuity.

The road from Cortes Bay to Squirrel Cove is gravel. It is rough in spots but easily passable. At Seaford Road, bear right, following the signs to Squirrel Cove, then turn left onto Squirrel Cove Road, which climbs before it dips down to the cove. From the high points of the road there are good views of the islands east of Cortes and the peaks of the mainland mountains.

Squirrel Cove is a quiet little community in a spectacular natural setting. It seems to be encircled by mountains rising to distant peaks that remain snow-topped even in the summer. Cottages cling to the shoreline near a store, and the Yaculta village is visible on the southeast shore of the cove. Squirrel Cove is popular with boaters for its natural beauty and protected anchorage. There is a government dock, boat launch, fuel pump, store with a liquor outlet and post office, and a seasonal arts and crafts outlet.

Past Squirrel Cove, the road climbs into the forested central island. There are about about 6 kilometres of gravel road, broken by small patches of paving where a few homes are grouped together, before this road joins the pavement at Gorge Harbour Road. Turn right here to return to your starting point at the ferry terminal.

What the Main Route Misses

Smelt Bay Provincial Park

This 16-hectare park is about 20 paved kilometres from the ferry landing, along Sutil Point Road. Located near the southern tip of Cortes, it has stunning views to the south and west, and access to a long pebble beach that curves around to Sutil Point. The point is named after the Spanish vessel *Sutil*, commanded by Captain Galiano, who explored this area in 1792. The more descriptive name Reef Point was given to the area by locals: shoals, studded with large boulders, extend for a kilometre southwest of the point. Facilities at the park include 23 campsites in the woods back from the beach, pit toilets, water and a picnic area. Rolling hills behind the beach are thought to have been trench embankments built by Salish Indians to defend against the marauding Yacultas.

Emergencies and Information

The Quadra Island RCMP are responsible for law enforcement on Cortes. Emergency numbers are listed in the front of the telephone directory, or you can call the operator, who will forward your call.

The Infocentre at Campbell River and business outlets on Cortes can provide information on local facilities and events.

Camping and Accommodation

Smelt Bay Provincial Park, with 23 campsites, is the only public campground on Cortes. Check local directories, the Infocentre in Campbell River, or Tourism B.C.'s *Accommodations* booklet for information on bed and breakfast establishments, resorts and motels on Cortes. Accommodation is limited, but there is not much tourism on the island.

Shopping and Services

Amenities at Whaletown, Mansons Landing, and Squirrel Cove include groceries, gas, propane, and post offices, and there is a liquor outlet at Squirrel Cove. Some supplies, and shower and laundry facilities, are also

Smelt Bay Provincial Park.

151

seasonally available at marinas at Gorge Harbour and Cortes Bay. The Mansons Landing Community Hall, with a daycare, North Island Community College, post office, cafe, lounge, library and nearby church and restaurant, provide a number of services for islanders and visitors. A few craft outlets and artists' studios are open to visitors.

Recreation and Events

Locals can offer information on fishing and cruising charters, as well as events such as community fairs, craft markets and festivals. Cortes Days are held each summer at Smelt Bay Provincial Park.

Hiking — Parks and Beaches

The north end of the island contains a number of forest trails, but the trails are unmarked. Locals may be able to give directions on trails to Carrington Lagoon, Barrett Lake and Von Donop Inlet, as well as other trails, most built on the remains of old logging roads. For less rugged walking, the road-accessible beaches of the southern part of the island provide interesting shoreside hikes with open vistas.

Mansons Landing Provincial Marine Park

Walking in Mansons Landing Park is more of an exploration than a vigorous hike, for there are several different environments to enjoy. From the government wharf in the park, you can walk south along the fine sandy beach of the foreshore, where loons and a variety of waterfowl swim along the offshore kelp beds. Sand dollars and the occasional moon snail shell lie among the debris at the high tide line. About a 25-minute walk from the government dock, watch for a huge granite boulder, where a petroglyph of a fish, almost 3 metres long, has been pecked into the rock.

Shoreline near Mansons Landing Provincial Marine Park.

The walk to Hague Lake — about 1 kilometre from the wharf — skirts the lagoon and passes through a forest.

Smelt Bay Provincial Park

The sand and pebble beach of this 16-hectare park leads to Sutil Point. The reef here can provide a fascinating few hours of walking at low tide, among the large boulders and tide pools. Wear appropriate footgear, as hiking over these large pebbles can be difficult.

Paddling and Small Boating — A Convoluted Coast

The indented shores and enclosed harbours of Cortes Island can give hours, days or a lifetime of enjoyable exploration for paddlers and small boaters. Tides run up to 4 knots through constricted entrances to inlets and harbours, however, so paddlers should consult current tables and use caution in these areas.

Gorge Harbour

Distance: 4.5 nautical miles. *Launching*: end of Robertson Road.

This harbour is almost completely enclosed and has many coves and islands to explore by small boat. It is protected from most winds, although westerlies blowing over the low-lying west arm of the harbour can produce a chop.

There are pictographs on the high cliffs at the narrow entrance to the harbour. They are best viewed at high water when the current is slack, as the tidal current runs at up to 4 knots through the shallow opening. It is thought that the pictographs, about half-way down the cliff wall, were made by lowering the artists on ropes from the top of the cliff. Stories tell of how the Gorge Harbour Indians ambushed a hostile band by balancing huge rocks on the edge of the cliff and releasing them as the invaders passed through the gorge.

Squirrel Cove

Distance: 4.5 nautical miles. *Launching*: Squirrel Cove government wharf.

One of the most beautiful anchorages in Desolation Sound, Squirrel Cove opens up to a large basin with many nooks and islands to anchor behind. Inside there are lots of opportunities for protected paddling among coves and inlets, islands and the lagoon. Moving tides form rapids at the narrow entrance to the lagoon, thought to be a "lake in the woods" by

18th century explorers. If you don't want to shoot the rapids, enter at slack tide. A canoe, dinghy or kayak are great for viewing the array of marine life in the still, warm waters of the lagoon.

Subtle Islands

Distance: 3 nautical miles return. *Launching*: Whaletown.

A favourite picnic and camping spot, these islands are known as Camp Island by locals. The tombolo connecting the islands is exposed at all but the highest tides. The name of the islands is the English translation of the Spanish "sutil."

Marina Island

Distance: variable. *Launching*: Whaletown or Manson's Landing.

Marina is a low-profile island lying in the lee of the western part of Cortes Island. The island was named by Captains Galiano and Valdes for a beautiful slave captured by Hernando Cortes, the Spaniard who conquered Mexico in 1520. She became Cortes's mistress and helped his campaign by providing information about Mexico. There's a lovely beach on the western side of Marina Island. Another favourite spot is a grassy area just inside Shark Spit. The tide flows through Uganda Passage at a rate of 2 to 3 knots, so paddlers putting in at Whaletown should consult tide and current tables and beware of winds.

Hague Lake

Distance: variable. *Launching*: off Quais Bay Road.

When it's blowing outside, Hague Lake is a great place for a calm paddle. The shoreline can be explored in a couple of hours. Gas motors are forbidden on the lake, which is the source of the community's drinking water, and bathers are asked not to use tanning lotions or shampoos and soaps. There are cutthroat trout here, so you might want to try your luck. A channel, navigable by canoe or kayak, connects Hague Lake to Gunflint Lake.

When You Arrive by Private Boat

Whaletown Bay

There is moorage at the government float at the south end of the bay and temporary anchorage throughout the bay. Fuel and water are available at the float, and food and other supplies at the General Store.

Cortes Bay

A government dock at Cortes Bay provides berthage space. There are also floats at the marina on the south shore, where fuel and other supplies can be obtained. The bay is fairly secure in most weather. You can move to the south shore if there is a strong southeasterly or southwesterly, and with a strong north wind the west end of the bay is best.

Gorge Harbour

Anchorage is available throughout Gorge Harbour, and there is moorage at the marina. The government wharf is small and often crowded. Supplies are available at the marina here, and it is less than 3 kilometres by paved road to Whaletown. The bay and its islands are interesting to explore by dinghy. At the farthest western tip, there is a local undeveloped picnic area. See the section on Paddling and Small Boating for more information on Gorge Harbour.

Mansons Landing Provincial Marine Park

This beautiful park has a number of attractions. There are fine sand beaches, and a public shellfish reserve assures a good supply of clams and oysters. Check Fisheries regulations for size and catch limits of shellfish. The lagoon is a great place to explore by dinghy. It is less than a 1-kilometre walk along a trail to the beach at Hague Lake. The park is not a completely safe anchorage, however, as it is exposed to the southwest. The government dock has limited moorage and is often full, but somewhat protected

Wharf at Mansons Landing Provincial Marine Park.

anchorage can be found behind Cat and Sheep islets. Local boats are sometimes anchored in the deep basin at the end of the lagoon, but access for most craft is limited to high water. Supplies such as groceries and fuel are available at a store near the government dock.

Squirrel Cove

This is one of the most popular anchorages in the Desolation Sound area, so if you are looking for solitude in the summer months, this is not the place for you. Squirrel Cove has abundant safe anchorage in its northern section. There are many protected byways to explore by dinghy. Tidal rapids run through the entrance to the large lagoon at the northern end of the cove. A government wharf is located on the south shore of Squirrel Cove and a nearby store sells supplies and gas. For more information on Squirrel Cove, see A Route to Follow and Paddling and Small Boating.

Coulter Bay

There is good protection from the prevailing westerlies in Coulter Bay. Shellfish are plentiful in the tidal flats at the end of the bay. A rough road through lush coastal rainforest leads to Whaletown Bay (about 3 to 4 kilometres), where there are supplies at a general store.

Carrington Bay

Temporary anchorage is available behind the islets in Carrington Bay but the bay is exposed to northwesterlies. It is interesting to explore the coastline here, which is protected by a recreational reserve. Energetic boaters could haul a small boat over a short land bridge which separates the bay from Carrington Lagoon.

Von Donop Inlet

This narrow, five-kilometre-long inlet comes within 800 metres of connecting with Squirrel Cove, on the east side of Cortes. The inlet is so narrow and twisting that anchorage is safe in all weather. There are several anchorages throughout the inlet, but many boaters choose to go to its head. Trails lead from here through the centre of the island, connecting with several lakes and Carrington Lagoon. The north arm of the inlet is a lagoon which can only be entered at high tide because of the swift current through its shallow, boulder-studded entrance.

Cortes Fishing

Marina Reef

Launching: Mansons Landing or Gorge Harbour.

The reef and kelp beds at its south end produce chinooks May to August when the bait is there. The reef is known for good coho fishing. Rockfish are caught year-round.

Coulter Bay.

157

Sutil Point

Launching: Mansons Landing, Gorge Harbour or Cortes Bay.

From May to July chinook gather here on the flood. Coho are caught from June to September.

Hague Lake

Launching: Quais Bay Road.

No motors are permitted on this lake, which is a drinking-water reservoir. You can launch just off Quais Bay Road, at the southeast end of the lake. There are plenty of cutthroat trout, with an average length of 40 centimetres. You can also fish in Gunflint Lake, entered by a channel from Hague Lake, but you should check the fishing regulations for both lakes before fishing there, as a catch-and-release regulation has been in effect for Gunflint Lake.

Cortes Scuba Diving

Gorge Harbour Narrows

Boat dive. Launching: Gorge Harbour.

The area around the entrance to Gorge Harbour provides good opportunities to see octopi and wolf-eels. The sheer rock walls of the gorge descend straight down to about 10 or 14 metres. Decorated warbonnets, grunt sculpins, nudibranchs and gunnels abound, providing plenty of opportunity for underwater photographers. The dive is best done at slack tide as the current can be swift through the narrow opening. There may not be air or diving facilities on Cortes, but air is likely available on Quadra and at Campbell River.

Malcolm Island

A Utopian Legacy

 Malcolm Island, 83-square-kilometres, lies in the cold, clear waters of Queen Charlotte Strait, at the northeast end of Vancouver Island. Its population of about 900 is concentrated in the small fishing village of Sointula, with a few homes clustered around Mitchell Bay.

Sointula is a tidy, picturesque village perched on the eastern arm of Rough Bay. An aura of calm and order pervades the village, and there is little evidence today of the many years of struggle and heartbreak that surrounded the beginning of the settlement.

The story of Sointula begins in the 1890s, when Finnish immigrants

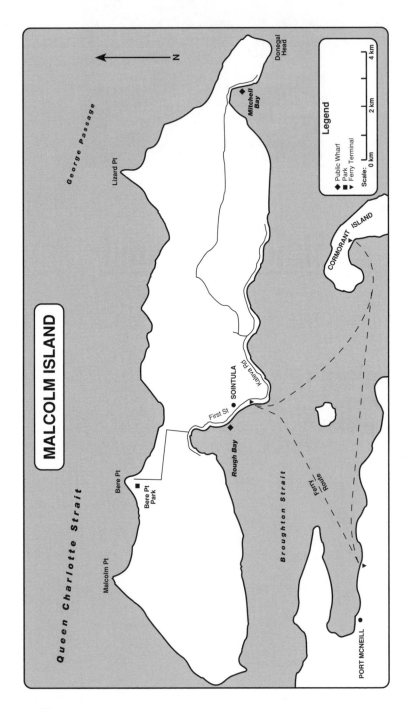

MALCOLM ISLAND

Legend

◆ Public Wharf
■ Park
▼ Ferry Terminal

Scale:
0 km — 2 km — 4 km

Queen Charlotte Strait

George Passage

Lizard Pt

Donegal Head

◆ Mitchell Bay

Kaleva Rd

SOINTULA ●

First St

◆ Rough Bay

Bere Pt

■ Bere Pt Park

Malcolm Pt

Broughton Strait

CORMORANT ISLAND

Ferry Route

PORT MCNEILL ●

working in James Dunsmuir's mines near Nanaimo became disillusioned with the poor working conditions and low wages. Safety precautions at the mines were almost nonexistent, and several men had died in an explosion. The Finns had come to Canada with high hopes for bettering their lives. They organized study groups and became familiar with the works of Matti Kurikka, a Finnish writer and lecturer. Kurikka's writings reflected his socialist ideals, stressing pacifism, universal suffrage, equality for women, education for all, and power to the people. He was interested in setting up a Utopian community that would embody his ideals, and when the Finns in Nanaimo asked him to come to Canada and help them, he readily agreed.

In August of 1900 Kurikka arrived in Canada and was made president of the group's board of directors. After poring over maps of the coast, they decided upon Malcolm Island and began the process of getting government approval for the Kalevan Kansa Colonization Company. Under the terms of the agreement between the government and the settlers, each settler would receive a 32-hectare (80-acre) parcel, to a total of 350 parcels. Ownership of the land would be granted after a period of seven years, provided it was improved to a value of $2.50 per acre. The Finns were to become British subjects and the children were to attend an English school built by the government. The settlers would be responsible for improvements such as roads and wharves. No taxes would be levied for the seven-year period, except for a poll tax of $3.00. Yearly reports were to be filed with the government and if the colony was successful, more land would be granted at the end of the seven-year period. With the signing of the agreement, the first hurdle was conquered.

The first settlers arrived at Malcolm Island in December, 1901, after a rough passage from Nanaimo by sailboat that took a week and a half. They were followed by a second group, including one woman, in January. That spring brought more settlers — including a doctor from Oregon — attracted by Kurikka's writings in the paper he had started in Nanaimo, *Aika*, and by his lecture tours throughout North America, where he urged people to join the colony.

Spirits were high in the summer of 1902, when the colonists gathered to celebrate their accomplishments and plan the guidelines for their community. Hoping to attract more colonists, the steamer *Capilano* had been chartered to bring a large group of interested families from the Nanaimo area. Those at the meetings agreed to begin logging near Mitchell Bay, a future sawmill site was selected and the townsite was planned. Work groups were organized and after much discussion, the work day was shortened to eight hours from the standard nine-hour day of the time. A name for the community was officially chosen: Sointula, the Finnish word for harmony. It seemed a most appropriate name that sunny summer, which held such great promise.

The enthusiasm was contagious, and most of the visitors remained in Sointula, spending the summer in tents. But with the onset of winter, problems beset the young community. Housing was woefully inadequate and settlers arriving in December shivered in tents while temporary housing was hastily constructed. The logging operation, run by tradesmen unfamiliar with the woods, did not run smoothly, and the donkey engine proved to be much too small and weak for the huge logs. The group acquired a seiner but the price of salmon was low. They obtained rights to build a cannery at Knight Inlet, on the opposite side of Queen Charlotte Strait, but were unable to build it due to outstanding debts. Meanwhile, Kurikka was continuing to attract new colonists to the undersupplied community. Cattle and horses were brought in, but had to be pastured on Vancouver Island. Feed was shipped over on the community's steamboat *Vinetta*, which brought back much-needed milk for the colonists on the return run. Eventually land was cleared on Malcolm and the livestock was installed in a large barn with a loft.

By 1903, the struggling community was deeply in debt. The share purchase of $200, vital for capital funds, was waived for those unable to pay, and labour was substituted. Unfortunately, there were no controls and too many couldn't pay. With debts already totalling $10,000, Kurikka was having difficulty raising further funds. Ironically, the community founded on principles of noncapitalist ideals was becoming more and more enslaved to a capitalist system through mounting debts.

That January, tragedy struck. A meeting had been called to discuss the financial situation with an investigator sent by the creditors. Almost all the settlers were present in the large three-storey community hall, the

Sointula shoreline.

adults in the top-floor meeting room, the children asleep on the lower level. Suddenly the call of "Fire!" was raised. Pandemonium ensued, as people leapt or were dropped from the third-storey windows. Parents tried vainly to find their children in the smoke-filled rooms. When the fire died down, the grieving community had lost two women, one man and eight children. Others were injured in the fall or severely burned.

A police investigation followed. It was determined that the fire had started in the heating pipes that led from the brick oven, but ugly rumours circulated that Kurikka and the board's secretary, Makela, had started the fire in order to obliterate the records and cover up irregularities in the bookkeeping.

Financial difficulties continued to plague the colony, which by the end of 1903 numbered 238. Every avenue — fishing, logging, or utilizing the skilled tradesmen in the colony — was blocked, either by lack of start-up capital, or depressed market prices. Debts were piling up and it was decided at the end of that year to mortgage buildings and machines to keep the colony afloat. Despite these difficulties, the colonists did not surrender their utopian vision. They organized a choir and band, gave plays and had discussion groups. In 1904, the first school was built by the settlers, in return for a land grant of 259 hectares (640 acres) in the townsite area. Around that time, the colony experimented with another idealistic innovation: a group home for the children, which would free mothers to work in the community. The idea foundered as most of the women wanted to keep their children at home.

In 1904, two events spelled the eventual demise of the Utopian community. In Vancouver bids were being sought for construction of bridges over the Capilano and Seymour rivers, and Kurikka's ill-advised bid, opposed by many in the community, won the contract. Members of the community laboured for several months with no wages to satisfy the contract and many left the community in despair.

Others were beginning to question Kurikka's leadership, both financially and idealistically — particularly his ideas on "free love." An advocate of freedom and equality for women, Kurikka saw marriage as a form of oppression for women of the day. Many in the community, conventionally married, were not happy that the outside world believed the community to unconditionally support Kurikka's ideas. In October 1904, faced with a group divided in its loyalty to him, Kurikka left, taking half the community with him. Some of those who left were worn out and disillusioned, having lost everything.

Those who stayed at Sointula struggled on, but the finishing blow came when a shipload of milled lumber that was destined to pay the interest on the mortgage and buy essential clothing for the colonists was seized by creditors. With no more options open to them, the colony was liquidated.

The land was returned to the government in return for a loan to pay off the remaining debts.

Somehow the spirit of Sointula managed to survive. Those settlers who chose to stay purchased land from the government as private settlers. In 1914, the population was estimated at about 250 people, many of them members of the original community. They worked in logging and fishing and continued to meet in the hall and organize cultural events such as plays and discussion groups. Despite the failure of Kurikka's utopian ideal, many of his ideas survived in the community. In 1909, the first cooperative store was started, with every member of the community participating. The present building was built in 1953.

Today the Finnish influence is still strong — and visible in the many saunas — but there are different cultural groups in Sointula. The mainstay of island economy is a major fishing fleet, protected behind long stone breakwaters. The role of logging in island economy is diminishing, and the concept of developing tourism on the island is just beginning to be seriously considered. It is far from the regular tourist routes, but the clean air and water, the peacefulness, and the opportunities for scuba diving, whale watching and fishing are becoming known to a small but growing number of travellers.

Malcolm Island is in a superbly scenic area. The views are sometimes obscured by fog, which contributes to the strong maritime flavour of Sointula. Summer fog usually lifts some time in the morning, but by September, it can last most of the day. On rare occasions, it is too rough for the ferry to make the passage from Port McNeill, but islanders are patient with the weather, which is the arbiter of daily life.

Malcolm Island fishing fleet.

It is possible to spend a day on Malcolm Island and take in many of the island sights. But the visitor with more time to spare will have quite a different experience on this gentle island where harmony is an integral part of the community.

Getting There

Ferries leave regularly from Port McNeill for Sointula, a 20-minute passage across Broughton Strait. Ferry schedules are available from B.C. Ferries or Travel Infocentres in Campbell River, Port McNeill or Port Hardy. Check local directories for information on float planes and water taxis.

A Route to Follow

Sointula's main route is about 11 kilometres of paved road along the shoreline. Probably the best way to start out is to turn left after disembarking from the ferry and stop just a few metres away at the general store. A community notice board on the outside wall of the store has a variety of announcements including a calendar of local events.

The main street is a narrow lane that winds along the water. The older houses, colourfully painted and set amid pretty fenced gardens, perch above the road. On the water side, fishing sheds, boatbuilding establishments, marine ways, cottages and wharves form a charming mixture permeated with a maritime flavour. Farther back, several tiers of

Old buildings and narrow laneway in Sointula.

streets rise from the water, with many modern homes and the occasional oldtimer.

Continue along the main road, preferably on foot, to get a real sense of the all-pervasive atmosphere of the fishing life. Almost everyone you meet will greet you in a friendly fashion.

Many reminders of the interesting past of Sointula can be seen in the museum. It does not keep regular hours but will be opened on request: the number to call is posted at the museum, and it is well worth a visit.

The museum was officially opened in 1973. The idea came from a group of women who had been collecting artifacts of the early settlers. When a visiting antique dealer wanted to buy the coffee-grinding machine from the Co-op Store (an extremely impressive machine, 1.2 metres tall, shaped like a coffee pot), it prompted the committee to obtain the grinder themselves, and to take a more serious approach to their collection. The display today is a fascinating array of tools, household goods and — surprisingly — paintings. One wall is dominated by a huge, stylized rendition of three figures leaving a sooty, factory-besmirched land (capitalist Finland). They are bearing a red flag to a green pastoral country with red and white cottages and neatly fenced yards. (These typically Finnish houses can be seen throughout Sointula today). A bust of Lenin shares space with the original school books used by the children of the first settlers. There is also a collection of natural artifacts from the beach and fishing lures and floats, as well as a rubbing of the only known petroglyph on the island.

Mural in Sointula Museum.

A number of stores and other retail outlets are on the main route. Past the main commercial area are extensive government wharves. When the boats are in, the wharves are a jungle of poles.

You can continue around the end of Rough Bay, which has wide mud flats at low tide, where a variety of birds can be spotted. There are only a few homes past this point before the road ends, and the last houses give way to dense coastal forest.

Retrace the route to the ferry terminal and continue along the water, past the residential area. After a few blocks you will reach the tidy, well-tended cemetery. The gravestones give a glimpse into island history and chronicle events such as the 1903 fire in which eleven lives were lost. The paved road continues for another 9 kilometres, but you will soon be out of the village itself. It's a nice route to walk or drive, following along the shoreline and overlooking Broughton Strait. A number of establishments along this road offer accommodations.

What the Main Route Misses

A peculiarity of Malcolm Island is the lack of street signs. It's probably related to the small number of streets, but it can make getting directions somewhat difficult. However, the island is so small that a few false starts won't slow you down much. To get to many of Malcolm Island's interesting places, logging roads must be used. Much of the island is crisscrossed with these roads, and it is fine to use them, but they must be driven with caution during working hours. The following directions are based on approximate distances.

Mitchell Bay

Mitchell Bay is at the southeast end of the island. There is a log-booming ground at the end of the bay, but it is still peaceful and incomparably lovely, with expansive views of outlying islands and the jagged mountain peaks of Vancouver Island. About 100 people live around Mitchell Bay in an eclectic variety of homes — some old, some new, and some an interesting combination.

To get to Mitchell Bay, turn to the right from the ferry dock and travel 3.3 kilometres along the main paved road. Turn left onto a gravel road, identified as a logging road, and bear right at all junctions after this. If you find yourself at the garbage dump after turning off the main road, you have missed your turn. It is 11 kilometres of rough road, but the end result is worth it.

The road finally comes out at the end of the bay, where a rock and pebble beach is lined with driftwood and evergreens. At the head of the bay is a small log booming ground and a log dump. A little farther on is the government wharf.

Where the road bears to the left, away from the water, there is a grassy area where cars can be parked. Among the smooth rocks and tangled driftwood are old sheds and derelict boats. At all except the highest tides the beach is walkable for several kilometres around its perimeter, and there are views of Cormorant Island to the north, Stubbs and other offlying islands, and peaks on Vancouver Island. Along the shoreline are grassy bluffs with ferns, vetch, thistle and daisies. Large driftwood logs offer easy walking. Watch for otters along the shore. Eagles come to the head of the bay as the tide retreats to snatch salmon entrails discarded by anglers. Cruise ships ply Cormorant Channel, fading like ghosts into the mist, their stentorian horns warning smaller, frailer craft out of their paths.

Bere Point Regional Park

For locals and others who want to get away from the business and bustle of downtown Sointula, Bere Point (pronounced Bare) provides a camping getaway. Eight campsites overlook Queen Charlotte Strait and the islands and peninsulas of the mainland. Firewood, pit toilets and picnic tables are provided. Some lucky campers may even find hammocks at their sites. There is a rustic charm to the campground. The fire pits (found elsewhere on the island as well) are modified logging truck wheels. Picnic tables are roughly constructed of planks laid over sections of log. There is a rough boat launch at the entrance to the park, suitable for cartoppers, and a picnic site has a covered area with tables and barbecue pits.

In late August the seine fishery adds its own charm to the beauty of Bere Point, when as many as 50 seiners might be working the waters offshore.

Access to the park may not be well marked — like other sites on Malcolm Island. To get to Bere Point, turn left from the ferry dock. After about 2.8 kilometres, turn right onto a paved road which soon becomes gravel. Proceed another 600 metres to a T junction, where a sign warns that you are on an active logging road. Turn left at this junction. (As you turn you will see a sign for the park to your left.) From here it is another 2.5 kilometres over gravel roads. Follow the signs, which are posted regularly from here on. The road may be rough, but is suitable for most vehicles. However, be prepared for scrapes and loud thumps if your car is heavily loaded or low-slung.

Emergencies and Information

There is an RCMP detachment on Malcolm Island. There are no medical facilities on the island, but there is a hospital at Alert Bay. Emergency numbers are listed in the front of the telephone directory, or you can call the operator for assistance.

Check Infocentres in Port McNeill or Port Hardy, or inquire at local businesses, for information about facilities and events on Malcolm Island.

Camping and Accommodation

A regional park at Bere Point, accessible by rough gravel road, has 8 campsites, pit toilets, picnic tables and fire pits. There is no fee for camping here. There are also private campgrounds, bed and breakfast establishments, and hotel and lodge accommodations. For current listings, check Infocentres or Tourism B.C.'s annual *Accommodations* booklet, described in Chapter One.

Shopping and Services

The Co-op Store near the ferry dock can fill most needs for groceries, hardware and souvenirs. The store also sells liquor. Arts and crafts stores, a gas station and other commercial establishments are all located within a block. The post office is on 2nd Street, just behind the Co-op Store. Dining facilities along the waterfront offer views of the bay.

Recreation and Events

Whale-watching trips, fishing charters and sailing excursions can be arranged on Malcolm Island — ask locals for details, or check for brochures at Infocentres in Port McNeill and Port Hardy. Tennis courts are located beside the Museum: instructions for use of the courts are at the Co-op Store. Many residents have horses and guided horseback-riding tours may be available — inquire locally.

Annual events include the Family Days Celebration, with food booths, races and horse competitions, held at the ball field in August, and the Winterfestival and Craft Fair in December.

Hiking — Scenic Seafront

There are few established hiking trails on Malcolm, and the logging roads are not particularly inviting, or may be in use. The beaches are excellent for hiking, and beachcombers will be happy with treasures brought in by the tide, including the occasional glass or wooden float. The barnacles that wash up here grow to enormous sizes, and large sea urchin shells can be found among the debris at the high tide line.

From the ferry, you can hike the beaches at the end of 1st Street, around Dickenson Point and along the shoreline facing Broughton Strait. The road parallels the shore for 9 kilometres, and there are numerous places to pull over and park a car. Beach walks at Mitchell Bay and Bere Point are described in What the Main Route Misses.

"Welcome" bench along a Sointula road.

Lizard Point

The land at Lizard Point has been secured for a new regional park, which may be developed in the 1990s. The trail to the park is being cleared: details of the route may be available from the Mount Waddington Regional District offices in Port McNeill, or from businesses in Sointula. Lizard Point is the site of a large midden and the only known petroglyph on Malcolm Island. A face has been carved into a rock, exposed only when the tide is low. According to the writings of turn-of-the-century ethnographer Franz Boas, this point was known as "Two Faces," but only one face is visible now. Stories told by early pioneers confirm that two faces once were visible.

Paddling and Small Boating — Hug the Shoreline

Rough Bay

Distance: variable. *Launching*: boat launch in Sointula.

This is an easy paddle for those who like to snoop around docks and waterfront areas. Launch in the village and paddle to Dickenson Point and back to Rough Bay. Take care to stay out of the path of the ferry and watch for fishboats near the docks. There are a number of wooden sheds falling into disrepair along the shore, many sheltering abandoned boats. Photographers can often be seen capturing the picturesque waterfront on film. The mud flats at the end of Rough Bay are a good place to watch water birds.

Mitchell Bay

Distance: variable. *Launching*: government wharf at the east side of the bay.

The shoreline of Mitchell Bay is a quiet paddle, but you can also go farther afield and paddle around to Donegal Head. Although the water may seem calm, it can be deceptive: Cormorant Channel can get very rough. The tidal stream runs at 2 knots in the channel and there may be whirlpools and eddies around the point. Tides run up to 6 knots across Cormorant Channel in Weynton Passage, something to keep in mind if you intend to explore the islands and islets south of Mitchell Bay. If the weather and tides permit, you can paddle to Lizard Point, another 4.3 nautical miles. From here there are panoramic views north and south down Queen Charlotte Strait. See the section on hiking for information about Lizard Point.

171

When You Arrive by Private Boat

As Desolation Sound, near Cortes and Quadra islands to the southeast, becomes more popular, a growing number of recreational boaters are seeking the waters farther north. There are government wharves at Sointula, along with a complete array of facilities, and at Mitchell Bay, which has good anchorage and a government dock, but no other amenities.

Mitchell Bay.

Malcolm Fishing

Mitchell Bay

Launching: Mitchell Bay government wharf.

There is a core group of campers with runabouts who trek annually to Mitchell Bay. They come from as far away as the Prairies, not only for the August salmon runs, but for the peace and tranquility of Malcolm Island. The salmon start in May with the bluebacks; pinks come in alternate years in July and August; chinook and coho from July to September. This is a good area for coho, which school up until September. The area alongside the kelp beds that line the western margin of the bay can be productive if winds prevent venturing farther afield. Trolling is the favoured method, with some driftfishing.

Donegal Head

Launching: Mitchell Bay government wharf.

Chinooks in the 9- to 18-kilogram range are taken here on occasion. The best time to fish is on an ebb tide, which forms a back eddy around the kelp beds off the point. Coho and pinks can be caught here as well.

Weynton Passage

Launching: Mitchell Bay government wharf.

Weynton Passage, just over 2 nautical miles southeast of Mitchell Bay, offers excellent blueback and coho fishing from May to September, and pinks when they are running. Start fishing at high tide and fish through to slack. The stronger the current the better the fishing, as long as you have the horsepower to handle the currents, which run up to 6 knots.

The reef around Stubbs Island, at the northern end of Weynton Passage, is most productively fished on an ebbing tide. Jigging for cod and rockfish can be productive in holes and ledges by the dropoff.

Malcolm Scuba Diving

The seas around Malcolm Island provide some of the best year-round scuba diving to be had, including Stubbs Island, which is known all over the world. The combination of cold, clear waters and active tidal currents (to 6 knots) in Weynton Passage produces an abundance of marine life, including basketstars, sponges, hydrocorals, soft corals, nudibranchs and anemones, as well as a wide variety of rockfish.

There are facilities for divers in Port McNeill, Telegraph Cove and elsewhere on Vancouver Island. On Malcolm Island, there is a good shore dive at Donegal Head, with a typical cross section of underwater life — sponges, anemones, coral, ling cod, greenling and rockfish.

Stubbs Island and Plumper and Stephenson islets have been proposed as an ecological marine reserve. The proposal includes approximately 416 hectares, of which 32 hectares is land. Its purpose is to preserve the marine life characteristic of a high-current marine ecosystem. Collecting by divers here is discouraged.

Cormorant Island

Preserving a Heritage

 Lying in Broughton Strait, the passage between Malcolm and Vancouver islands, is tiny, crescent-shaped Cormorant Island. Just 6.5 square kilometres — almost 5 kilometres long and less than a kilometre wide — Cormorant Island has a remarkably rich history, preserved in two museums that tell of native and European settlement.

Many visitors to Cormorant and Malcolm islands are surprised to find that these two communities, in close proximity geographically and served by the same ferry out of Port McNeill, are so vastly different in atmosphere. While an aura of calm surrounds the comings and goings on Sointula, Alert Bay bustles with a constant stream of vehicle and pedestrian traffic along

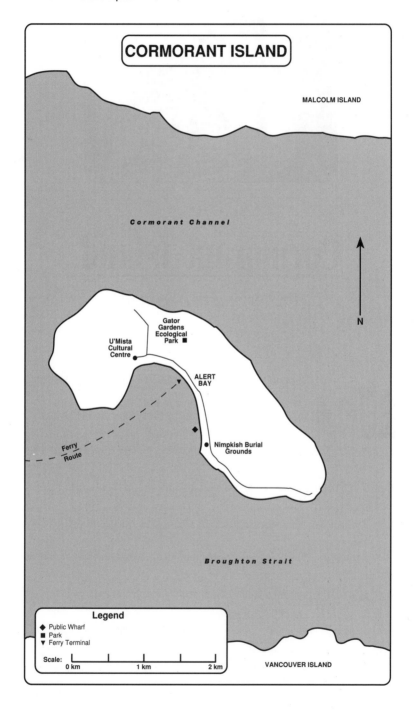

CORMORANT ISLAND

MALCOLM ISLAND

Cormorant Channel

N

Gator
Gardens
Ecological
Park ■

U'Mista
Cultural
Centre ●

ALERT
BAY

● Nimpkish Burial
Grounds

*Ferry
Route*

Broughton Strait

Legend
◆ Public Wharf
■ Park
▼ Ferry Terminal

Scale:
0 km   1 km   2 km

VANCOUVER ISLAND

its commercial waterfront area. Fishing and service industries are the mainstay of the island, and there is a thriving tourism industry, attracted by the native culture, and the opportunities for sport fishing and whale watching nearby. Alert Bay is also on the path of huge liners cruising the Inside Passage to Alaska, and the ships often stop here for the day. Full-size tour buses can even be seen rolling off the ferry.

The community of Alert Bay has a population of more than 1,300 and comprises the Municipality of Alert Bay and the Nimpkish Indian Reserve. Native and white groups cooperate today in community affairs, but it hasn't always been so peaceful. The banning of traditional potlatches, the confiscation of ceremonial regalia and the imprisonment of protesters is a chapter in coastal history that continues to shape events at Alert Bay to this day. The grim face of the old residential school dominates the harbour — now the Nimpkish Band office, the building is a symbol both of past difficulties and native hopes for the future.

Permanent settlement began on Cormorant Island when the huge sockeye runs of the Nimpkish River, on Vancouver Island 3 kilometres southwest of Alert Bay, caught the eye of S.A. Spencer and W. Huson — two entrepreneurs who proposed to build a cannery to take advantage of the phenomenal salmon runs. Finding the waters at the mouth of the river too shallow for the cannery, they leased Cormorant Island. By 1870, they brought in their first load of supplies for the establishment of a saltery.

Nimpkish Valley natives were employed in the saltery, but Spencer and Huson had difficulty in persuading them to stay in Alert Bay. To encourage permanent native settlement and provide their cannery with a steady supply of labour, Huson and Spencer suggested that Alfred James Hall of the Church Missionary Society move his mission from Fort Rupert, near present-day Port Hardy, to Alert Bay. In 1878, Hall was established in Alert Bay, bringing his pupils and their families with him.

From the beginning, Alert Bay natives resisted the strictures placed on them by white laws, particularly the federal banning of potlatches in 1884. This issue was to climax in the 1920s, under the administration of the Indian agent William Halliday.

Among coastal Indians, the potlatch was a complex system of distributing wealth and establishing a hierarchy of power. Halliday, who had the difficult task of administering the directions of the Department of Indian Affairs, also believed the potlatches to be detrimental to native life, taking their time, wasting their wealth, and preventing them from achieving the goal of assimilation.

From 1914 to 1920 he waged war on the custom, bringing charges against several people in Alert Bay. In 1921, it all came to a head with the Christmas Tree Potlatch, held some 25 kilometres to the east, on Village Island, where hundreds of Kwakiutl gathered from Cape Mudge, Alert Bay and Village Island. The gathering was reported to the agent and many people were arrested. A trial was held in the schoolhouse; the accused, sleeping on the floor at night, were guarded by RCMP officers.

E.K. DeBeck, son of a former Indian Agent, was counsel for the defense. Those on trial were given an option: if they would sign an agreement to give up potlatching and dancing, and would turn over all their ceremonial possessions, to be placed in Canadian museums, they could avoid a jail

Memorial poles overlook harbour in native burial ground.

sentence. Most agreed to the terms.

After the trial, the masks and other regalia, as well as coppers (flat sheets of beaten copper, from 15 centimetres to nearly a metre in height, cut in the shape of a shield and sometimes incised with the owner's crest) were collected at Halliday's home in Alert Bay, then shipped to Ottawa. Acting on his own initiative and against instructions, Halliday unwisely sold some of the gear to a New York museum for about $200, with the money to go to the owners of the property. The rest was shipped to Ottawa, but several pieces were missing when the crates were unpacked.

Probably one of the most revealing accounts of his years as Indian Agent at Alert Bay are found in Halliday's book, *Potlatch and Totem*, published in 1935, in which he outlines his position and expresses the tenor of the times.

In the 1970s, after years of effort by natives of Alert Bay and Cape Mudge, the federal government agreed to repatriate the property that had been seized, on the condition that the collection be housed in suitable museums. The result is the U'Mista Cultural Centre, where artifacts and the potlatch collection are displayed, and native history and traditions are being revived. With its mandate to collect, repatriate and restore not only the artifacts, but the cultural and artistic activities and historic records of the Kwakwaka'wakw (Kwakiutl) people, the cultural centre has become an integral part of the community. (See the Quadra Island chapter for a description of the museum at the Cape Mudge village.)

The cultural centre, the mortuary poles overlooking the harbour, and the Big House and totem pole attract a great number of visitors each year. Perhaps nowhere else on the south coast is the presence of the native community felt so strongly.

Getting There

B.C. Ferries operates a service from Port McNeill to Sointula and Alert Bay. Check with B.C. Ferries or Infocentres in Port McNeill and Port Hardy for schedule information. Check telephone directories for information on airlines serving Alert Bay. Local businesses and Infocentres can provide information about taxis, which are plentiful.

A Route to Follow

In Alert Bay, the main route is practically the only route. The island has less than 20 kilometres of road, virtually all of which is paved. Despite the small number of roads, traffic is fairly heavy, from large tour buses to car and truck traffic.

You can see most of the points of interest on Cormorant by staying on the main street that runs along the water. The town is so small that you will probably want to park your car or leave it in Port McNeill. About a half-block from the ferry terminal, the former firehall, recognizable by its tower which was once used to hang the hoses, houses an art gallery, the Travel Infocentre, and the municipal hall. Paintings in the gallery include a collection by B.C. artist Chris Nancarrow. The watercolours depict a year and a day in the life of Alert Bay's main street, from the U'Mista Cultural Centre to the residential area at the end of Fir Street. Just outside is a small paved rest area with benches overlooking the busy harbour.

There are gift shops, restaurants, inns and pubs right on this main stretch of road. Farther along, a large white building dominates the street. Built in 1925 to replace the original hospital dating from 1909, it was once the hospital and is now the nurses' residence; behind it are the buildings of the modern St. George's Hospital.

The small chapel with beautiful stained glass windows beside the hospital dates from 1925. The bible from the old St. Michael's School, dated 1850, is kept in the chapel, which is open to the public during the summer. Nearby is the Alert Bay Library and Museum, with its small but fascinating collection of artifacts and photographs from the early days of Alert Bay.

The museum also pays tribute to the art and life of Chief Henry Speck, one of the last hereditary chiefs on the coast. The story is told of how the talent of Henry Speck's grandfather, a respected artist, was passed on to Henry. When Henry was born, the umbilical cord was wrapped in a hide, and when the grandfather painted or carved, he wore the hide-wrapped cord on his wrist so that his talent and skill would be transmitted to his grandson. Chief Speck became internationally known for his paintings and was a respected leader in his community. One of his last paintings, *Killer Whale*, hangs in the museum. It was given to MV *North Island Princess*; when the ship ceased service in 1979, the painting was returned to the people of Alert Bay.

Ferry at Alert Bay.

One of Alert Bay's most solemn and impressive sights is the Nimpkish burial grounds, located next to the museum. The memorial poles in the native cemetery are a reminder of the dignity and mystery of the native culture. One of the most powerful tribes on the coast, the Alert Bay native community has been active in the fight to preserve that culture. Numerous totem poles, made by some of the area's best carvers, face the harbour. Visitors should use the sidewalk past the cemetery and not trespass on the burial grounds, which are Indian Reserve. In the summer of 1990, the Nimpkish Band blocked the road running past the graveyard to vehicle traffic, stating that the road had been laid over early gravesites.

Past the burial ground are the shipyards. The original building here dates from 1908 and was started by Spencer Huson, the son of W. Huson, who first settled Alert Bay.

The road winds along the waterfront past a variety of commercial establishments. Eventually it dwindles to a single row of homes. To continue the main route, return along Fir Street.

The tidy white fence and ornate trim of Christ Church have brightened Alert Bay since 1879, making it possibly the oldest structure on the island. The church was prefabricated in England and brought around the horn to be reassembled under the watchful eye of Reverend Hall. Hymns and prayers are said in both the native Kwak'wala and in English. One of the windows commemorates the first hundred years in Alert Bay, portraying Christ Church, St. Michael's School, St. George's Hospital, the mission ship *Columbia*, and the canoe which brought Reverend Hall to Alert Bay.

Christ Church, built in 1879.

The U'Mista Cultural Centre is at the western extension of the main route. The name derives from the word for the return of something valuable or important, and the stated aim of the cultural centre is to "u'mista" the history, language and culture of the Kwakwaka'wakw people. (See the introduction to this chapter for background information about the cultural centre.)

The showpiece of the museum is the gallery housing the repatriated potlatch collection, which is designed and built like a traditional big house. Years of petitioning the government to have the property returned to its owners bore results when the federal government agreed to its return on condition that it be housed in an appropriate facility. The society was incorporated in 1974 and the building opened in 1980.

The masks are not behind glass but in an open exhibit, increasing the power of the collection. Among the masks are storyboards that tell of the fight to maintain the dances and potlatches.

Visitors to the museum can watch videotapes that tell of the history of the museum and the struggle to have the artifacts returned, as well as the celebration accompanying their return. They underline in a moving way the determination of the Alert Bay natives to fight for their cultural heritage. A videotape that celebrates the life and work of local artist Mungo Martin, a man who bridged both cultures and was instrumental in helping to preserve traditional dances and songs, is also available for viewing.

The huge ghostly-looking bulk of the old St. Michael's residential school is next to the community centre. The first residential school was built in 1894. This one replaced it in 1929, and was designed to accommodate

U'Mista Cultural Centre.

200 students. In 1965 a new school was built and the old building is now the Nimpkish Band office.

What the Main Route Misses

Gator Gardens

A short walk up the hill from the ferry is an interesting ecological park known as Gator Gardens.

If you are travelling on foot, take the stairs near the ferry dock. The stairs were once the site of a conveyer belt that transported coal from where it was dumped near the shore to a wireless station established in 1912. The station is now a Ministry of Transport site, which handles mayday calls and weather reports. Go along Alder Street to the campground. Turn left past the campground to a public rest area with picnic tables, where the trails through the ecological gardens start.

Gator Gardens consists of woodland paths through dense coastal rainforest and the main attraction — a marshy area created when B.C. Packers built a dam to provide fresh water for their saltery. The water killed an area of cedar forest, leaving tall jagged snags and moss-draped stumps, but the marsh allowed a variety of other life to flourish. The spires of dead fir and cedar rise eerily from the swamp and the hoarse cries of ravens punctuate the stillness. A boardwalk winds through the marsh and connects with the network of forest trails. Ravens perch like sentinels and flutter from tree to tree, seeming to monitor the progress of intruders. The walk will take a total of about half an hour.

World's Tallest Totem Pole

Taller than all the structures at Alert Bay, this slim spire is reportedly the world's tallest totem pole, at almost 53 metres. In 1973, four years after the tree was felled and carefully lowered to the ground, Kwakwaka'wakw (Kwakiutl) carvers of various tribes spent six weeks carving the intricate figures depicting the history of the Kwakwaka'wakw nation.

The creation and raising of the pole was a community effort that united the village of Alert Bay. The raising was a tense affair that used a crew of over a dozen men. It was made even more difficult because an extension had been spliced to the tip of the pole when it was discovered that it had to be lengthened in order to qualify as the world's tallest totem pole. Until the last moment, some were predicting that the extension would snap off.

The pole is located near the Big House. To get there, turn right just before the band office and the U'Mista Cultural Centre, and proceed along Park Street. The pole will be visible ahead and to your left. There is a large parking lot by the pole.

The Big House was completed in 1963, and is used by people from many other villages for potlatches. The potlatch has been open to visitors, but with the return of stricter observance of the old customs, that may no longer be the case. Traditionally, potlatches are an integral part of the native Indian spiritual life and there is a strict protocol for participation.

Boardwalk through the swamp at the ecological park called Gator Gardens.

Emergencies and Information

There is an RCMP detachment on Cormorant Island, as well as St. George's Hospital. Emergency numbers are listed at the front of the telephone directory, or the operator can forward your call.

The Travel Infocentre in Alert Bay keeps regular hours, and local stores and businesses can also provide information about the island.

Camping and Accommodation

The Municipality of Alert Bay has a campground, Oceanview Campsite, about 1 kilometre by road from the ferry dock (by foot it is about half that distance). The campground has 12 sites, some serviced, and has flush toilets and showers. The sites have picnic tables, but there are no trees for attaching tent guywires or to provide privacy.

Hotels and bed and breakfast establishments, as well as cottages, offer a variety of accommodation. For current listings, check Tourism B.C.'s *Accommodations* booklet, described in Chapter One, or the Infocentres at Port McNeill and Port Hardy.

Shopping and Services

Alert Bay is well supplied with commercial establishments — gift stores, an art gallery, gas station, liquor store, grocery stores, clothing stores, hairdressers, pubs, a laundromat, and restaurants. A Royal Canadian Legion, community centre, post office and several churches serve the community.

Recreation and Events

Alert Bay has a movie theatre, bowling alley and tennis courts. The annual Sea Festival is held in August, with herring skiff races, displays of arts and crafts, contests such as the regatta, and a boat parade, as well as a salmon barbecue. In June, native celebrations include a soccer tournament and Salmon Princess Pageant.

Hiking — Waterfront Walks

There are few public hiking trails on Cormorant, other than the trails through the ecological park called Gator Gardens, which can be covered in about half an hour (see What the Main Route Misses for more information on the park). However, there is pleasant hiking along the waterfront, with its clear water and beautiful views. At low tide the shoreline east of the village can be hiked to the north side of the island. Poplar Road also leads to the north side, where a few hardy souls swim in the permanently frigid waters. Beachcombing can yield treasures such as floats and large shells. Huge driftwood burls and tree roots, some with large rocks embedded in

Government dock in Alert Bay.

them, show the force of winter winds along here. Offshore, ubiquitous kingfishers flash and dive and kelp beds that parallel the shore provide perching places for gulls.

Paddling and Small Boating — Around Town

The Shores of Cormorant

Launching: At the waterfront by the government dock. *Distance*: 6.5 nautical miles.

The shores around Cormorant Island can be an interesting day expedition. Tidal streams, however, run at 1 to 3 knots in the passage between Cormorant and Vancouver Island, and up to 4 knots between Gordon Bluff and the Pearse Islands. Paddlers should be familiar with the currents: there have been numerous incidents of novice paddlers having to be rescued from Johnstone Strait.

Around Leonard Point, winds combined with tides can make for dangerous conditions and there are no bays that offer protection from the dominant summer westerlies.

In Alert Bay harbour, care must be taken to stay out of the path of the ferry, as well as commercial fishboats and other motorized craft. Watch for wash from larger vessels.

When You Arrive by Private Boat

The only anchorage on Cormorant Island is in Alert Bay Harbour. There is a government dock, as well as a number of private floats. All amenities

Fishboat in Cormorant Channel.

187

are available in the village. During the season, ships cruising the Inside Passage stop at Alert Bay, their passengers adding to the bustle in the small town.

Fishing, Scuba Diving and Whale Watching

Cormorant Island is located in what many regard as one of the best regions in the world for fishing, scuba diving and whale watching. Fishing and whale watching charters are available on Cormorant Island and there are several scuba diving operations on nearby Vancouver Island. See the chapter on Malcolm Island for more specific information on fishing near Cormorant.

Other Books
of Interest

Andersen, Doris. *Evergreen Islands*. Vancouver: Whitecap Books, 1979.

Anderson, Aili. *A History of Sointula*.

Baikie, Wallace. *Rolling with the Times*. Campbell River, B.C.: 1985.

Bentley, Mary and Ted. *Gabriola: Petroglyph Island*. Victoria: Sono Nis Press, 1981.

Chettleburgh, Peter. *An Explorer's Guide to the Marine Parks of British Columbia*. Vancouver: Whitecap Books, 1985.

Corrigal, Margery. *The History of Hornby Island*. Hornby Island, 1978.

Cramond, Mike. *Salmon Fishing British Columbia, Volume I, Vancouver Island*. Surrey, B.C.: Heritage House, 1989.

Herger, Bob; Neering, Rosemary. *The Coast of British Columbia*. Vancouver: Whitecap Books. 1989.

Isbister, Winnifred A. *My Ain Folk: Denman Island 1875 - 1975*. Comox Valley: E.W. Bickle, Ltd., 1976.

Lewis-Harrison, June. *The People of Gabriola*. Gabriola Island, B.C., 1982.

MacIsaac, Ron; Clark, Don; Lillard, Charles. *The Devil of De Courcy Island, The Brother XII*. Victoria: Porcepic Books, 1989.

Mason, Elda, Copley. *Lasqueti Island: History and Memory*. South Wellington, B.C., 1976.

Merriman, Alec; White, Charles; Colegrove, Bruce. *Where to Find Salmon*. Sidney, B.C.: Saltaire Publishing, 1977.

Obee, Bruce. *The Gulf Islands Explorer*. Vancouver: Whitecap Books, 1990.

Obee, Bruce. *The Pacific Rim Explorer*. Vancouver: Whitecap Books, 1986.

Stormwell, Brad. *The Undiscovered Islands, Denman and Hornby Isle*. 1984.

Wolferstan, Bill. *Cruising Guide to British Columbia, Volume I, The Gulf Islands*. Vancouver: Whitecap Books, 1987.

Wolferstan, Bill. *Cruising Guide to British Columbia, Volume II, Desolation Sound*. Vancouver: Special Interest Publications, 1980.

About the Author

Since 1981 Elaine Jones has worked quietly behind the scenes in the publishing industry as editor of dozens of books. She has guided authors from manuscript to published work, and has played a significant editorial role in the production of such award-winning books as *The Forests of British Columbia* and *Married to the Wind, A Study of the Prairie Grasslands*. Her writing is published in western Canadian magazines and travel books. *The Northern Gulf Islands Explorer* is her first full-length book, a welcome addition to the Whitecap 'Explorer' series.

The mother of two grown children, Linnea and Jed, she divides her time between her Vancouver home, where she lives with her husband, David Parkin, and a cottage on the Northern Gulf Islands. A seasoned beachcomber, camper and paddler, she travels between writing and editing assignments.